2,50

NEIGHBORS TO THE SOUTH

BOTAFOGO BAY, RIO DE JANEIRO, BRAZIL

NEIGHBORS
to the SOUTH

by DELIA GOETZ

ILLUSTRATED WITH PHOTOGRAPHS

HARCOURT, BRACE AND COMPANY
NEW YORK

TABLE OF CONTENTS

LIST OF ILLUSTRATIONS

ix

xi

FOREWORD

For centuries the people of the United States and the people of the other American countries went their respective ways with very little association or knowledge of each other. Great distances, inadequate communications and language differences kept them apart. When the man from Buenos Aires, Rio de Janeiro, or Lima, traveled abroad he usually went to Europe—and the same was true of the citizen of Boston, Chicago, or Kansas City. However, in recent years, all of this has been changing with increasing rapidity. Excellent steamships now ply between the United States and both the east and west coasts of South America. The finest and swiftest of airplanes link the capital cities of the other Americas with the leading communities of our own country. Trade between Latin America and the United States has mounted steadily. These and other forces are creating a growing sense of community of interests among the twenty-one American nations.

Almost by instinct with the rise of totalitarian militarism in Europe the American states drew together for co-operation and mutual assistance in defense against what was felt to be a common danger. The "Good Neighbor" policy became a reality in the relations of governments. Inter-American conferences one after another reached agreements whereby our cooperative efforts might be made more effective. Today there is more of confidence and good will among the American governments than ever before.

But it is not enough that governments shall follow the "Good Neighbor" policy; it is fully as important that the people of the twenty-one American nations shall become good neighbors. In other words we must get acquainted. Next to meeting people on their own soil the best way to get acquainted is to study about them. Fortunately the schools and colleges of our country are sensing the importance of helping students to understand their neighbors to the south. But unfortunately there are not nearly enough good books available. A common error of much of the existing literature has been to lump the twenty other Americas together and label the compound Latin America. Small wonder that so many of us in the United States have such inaccurate conceptions of our neighboring countries and their peoples.

This mistake the present volume avoids. Each country is considered separately. With a rare discrimination the essential facts about the geography, climate, and the people—who they are and how they make a living—are brought out. Just enough of the romantic is introduced to give the reader a "feeling" for the life in each country studied. In fact the impression left by reading this delightfully interesting and instructive little book is similar to that left by an airplane trip around South and Central America. One has formed only a speaking acquaintance with the respective countries and yet the charm and distinctive qualities of every one of them are so intriguing he longs to return to each for a good long stay. Pending the time when the return journey may be possible he turns to books for a more thorough study of the several countries. Like seeing a new world for the first time from a plane as we journey from country to country, in this volume scenes of mountains, valleys, streams, cities, and people pass before our eyes; people so quaintly different and yet basically so like ourselves. And with these fascinating but tantalizing brief glimpses there comes a desire to know more about the places and the people in them. If as a result of this experience the reader resolves that some day he will visit these neighboring lands and then goes straight away to the library for further reading, I am certain that the author's highest purpose in writing the book will have been realized.

BEN M. CHERRINGTON
*Adviser to the Division of Cultural
Relations, Department of State*

NEIGHBORS TO THE SOUTH

1

INTRODUCTION TO THE AMERICAS

ON a bright summer day a huge plane roared in from the Caribbean and settled down on the blue waters at Miami. The boy who was the first passenger to land had finished breakfast three days before in a sunny garden in Brazil. Today he was in time for a mid-afternoon lunch in the United States. The other meals he had eaten in several different countries, and hundreds of miles separated the two beds in which he had slept.

He had never seen the countries over which the droning plane sped him. He remembered them now as a confused jumble of jungle and parched desert, sprawling mountain ranges whose sharp peaks the watchful pilot had dodged, and palm-fringed islands dotting the Caribbean Sea. Now and then he had

3

caught a glimpse of cities and villages. Beyond them he saw homes and fields. He was curious to know more about them and the people who lived there. What grew in the fields that stretched off into the horizon? he wondered.

Most of us have the same jumbled picture of the countries beyond our southern border. We call them neighbors, yet we know little about the people and countries in the other Americas—the vast land stretching from the palms and cane fields of Cuba to the penguins and snowfields of Little America. To most of us they seem strange and far away.

But it is important for us to know more about our neighbors on this hemisphere. Like the boy in the plane we are interested in the people who grow our breakfast coffee and cocoa, our bananas and sugar, and the chicle for our chewing gum. On every side, too, we hear that the safety and happiness of the United States and the other American nations depend upon working together. Like players on a team, nations can do better teamwork if they know each other.

To describe the twenty countries of Latin America is

AIRPLANE VIEW OF RIO DE JANEIRO, BRAZIL

as difficult as to describe twenty different people. Many of us have thought that these southern countries are alike because we group them all under the same name —Latin America. But just as we speak of Kentuckians and Iowans and Californians, the people of Latin America prefer to be called Brazilian, Costa Rican, or Mexican. And those three countries are as different

5

from each other as they are from us. Sometimes we speak of the other Americas as "Spanish America." But the people of Brazil, the largest country of the twenty, speak Portuguese and are often annoyed at the number of Spanish letters they receive. The natives on the island of Haiti speak French. The official language of the other eighteen countries is Spanish, although six of these have more Indians than whites, and many of the Indians can speak little or no Spanish. The people are of different races, too. Some, like the citizens of Argentina, Costa Rica, and Uruguay, are almost entirely white. Some countries, like Brazil, have a mixture of white, Indian, and Negro. Haiti is all black.

In size the Americas vary from tiny Salvador, about the size of Maryland, to Brazil, so big that all of the United States could be dropped inside and still there would be room for a second state of Texas. Mexico is a fourth as large as the United States, and Nicaragua is about the size of England. Together they are about three times as large as the United States, but their population—less than our own—spreads thinly over their territory.

6

PLANE FLYING OVER THE ANDES

These countries have many differences, yet they are alike in many ways. Years ago, when one of the Spanish conquerors returned to Spain, the king asked him to describe this new world that had been claimed for the Spanish Crown. In answer the conqueror took a piece of paper, crushed it in his hand, and placed it on the table before the king. It was an apt descrip-

7

tion, and with two or three exceptions it applies to each separate nation as well as to Latin America as a whole. Most of the countries have high cool plateaus; many have mountain ranges with peaks snow-capped the year around. All of them have low green valleys, and sometimes hot, lush jungles.

There are lots of tall tales about the climate of Latin America. Most of them are told by people who have never been there! Because these countries are south of us, there is a general belief that they are hot. But altitude also has a great deal to do with climate. Parts of New Mexico and Arizona, for instance, are very hot in July and August, but within a few hours' drive into their mountains the climate will be delightfully cool and comfortable. The same is true in Latin America. Even Ecuador, straddling the equator, is so high that much of it has a comfortable climate in which to live. And if you spend midsummer in the Guatemalan highlands, you will be glad to find a hot water bottle tucked in your bed at night. Almost half the people in the other Americas live at an altitude where the year-round climate is as agreeable as that of any place

BRAZILIAN JUNGLE

in the world. It is true that there are also dense hot jungles where it is an effort to move about at all; and the southern parts of Chile and Argentina are so damp and cold that only hardy Indians care to live there. But it would be just as incorrect to say that Latin America is all cold and damp as it is to say, as one so often hears, that it is frightfully hot.

The Indians of Latin America are quite different from our own. At the time of the Spanish conquest, few of the natives in the countries beyond the Rio Grande were roving, fishing, and fighting Indians. They tilled the soil, worked the mines, and made beautiful handicraft. They were good architects and built magnificent temples to their gods. They constructed roads that even today haven't been surpassed, and they had a well-developed system of government in their tribes. After the conquest they were pressed into the services of their conquerors. Today in all but half a dozen of the Latin American nations the pure Indian and the *mestizo*—Indian and white mixed— are increasing in number. Most of them are still laborers who till the soil, dig the mines, bear the burdens,

MAP OF THE AMERICAS

and form the rank and file of the army. In some countries—Mexico, for instance—the Indian is slowly beginning to take his place as a part of the nation. But for Latin America the problem of the Indian and his place in the country is a difficult one on which many men for many years have been thinking and working

2

ON THE ISLANDS—CUBA, HAITI, DOMINI-CAN REPUBLIC

I LIKE you better now that I'm used to you," a frank little Cuban boy once told his American teacher. Cubans and the people of our own country have had an opportunity to know each other. The island is only ninety miles from the southernmost point of Florida. Planes hop over from Miami in less than two hours, and the boat from Key West makes the trip in seven.

"Pearl of the Antilles" the island is often called because of its beauty. But its immense sugar cane fields have earned it the title of "The World's Sugar Bowl." Like a sea of green the great cane fields stretch over thousands of acres. The overseer lives near by in his large house with its wide verandas, surrounded by fragrant gardens. Early in the morning when the dew is still on the fields, he rides out through a lane lined with tall palm trees to look over the plantation and supervise the work there. All year round the work goes on. Sometimes the men clear and burn off the land for new fields. Or perhaps they are planting short young cane shoots that soon turn into pale green feathery cane that ripples like water when the wind blows over it. At night in the moonlight, the fields look like vast sheets of silver.

When the cane is ready for cutting, work speeds up on the plantation. There is no time to waste, and hundreds of laborers are brought in from Haiti and Jamaica to cut the cane. Ever since Cuba's first cane fields were planted centuries ago, the Negro has worked them. Carrying murderous-looking knives (*machetes*) they move through the tall, green cane. With one stroke they cut the stout round stalks of cane, slash off the feathery tops, and toss them onto a heap near by. Night and day during the cutting season, the mills keep grinding. Night and day big caterpillar carts drawn by lumbering oxen keep a moving

CAPITOL BUILDING IN HAVANA, CUBA

chain between plantation and freight cars that haul the cane to the mill. Sometimes the men sing as they work, strange, lonely chants their forefathers sang long ago in Africa.

The laborers' huts huddle together in little villages here and there on the huge plantations. Usually they have one room, an earthen floor, and a grass roof.

15

Sometimes the walls are made of grass, woven or thatched. They are poor little homes, but protection against rain and, now and then, a cold wind that sweeps down from the north for a brief stay in Cuba. But the days are usually warm. Vegetable gardens surround the houses and a few chickens and a turkey or two scratch in the dooryard. The larger villages have a store, usually a school and a church. Resting from their labors in the cane fields, the Negroes make merry on their holidays. No colors are too bright for their costumes and no music too difficult for their dancing feet to follow.

Sugar has made good times and bad times in Cuba. Many millions of dollars have been made on sugar and as many millions have been lost. During the World War of 1914 to 1918, when European beet fields were trampled by the marching feet of soldiers, sugar was scarce, the price was high, and Cuba was prosperous. Steadily the price rose until it had doubled and trebled. Land owners rushed to plant more cane in the fields that had grown food for the island—beans, corn, and vegetables. The war went on and their for-

THE PRADO, HAVANA, CUBA

tunes swelled. Fantastic tales are still told in Cuba of how this wealth was spent. Whole families—and big ones—went to New York, Paris, or London and rented entire floors at the best hotels. When the cold winter days came, some of them fled back to the balmy island. Those who stayed in Havana built homes like palaces and furnished them like movie sets, with beautifully carved furniture, rich paintings, and tapestries. An army of gardeners kept each plant in the formal gardens surrounding these mansions trained and in place. Snow-white aigrettes and long-legged flamingos admired their reflections in the quiet waters of pools. "The Dance of the Millions" is the way Cubans refer to those days.

But when the war ended and Europe began to cultivate her fields, the price of sugar dropped as suddenly as it had risen. Millions of dollars were lost overnight. Distress and despair spread through the island. Wages dropped or stopped entirely. Laborers had no money to buy expensive imported food. Everything had been planted to cane. Even beans and rice were imported.

Wise from this experience, Cuba has planted other

CUBAN SUGAR CANE FIELD

crops to make it less dependent on sugar. Canning factories pack pineapples, guavas, tomatoes, and other vegetables. A condensed milk plant and a yeast factory are both doing a thriving business. Growing herds of cattle and hogs may bring the price of meat within the budget of the laborer.

Cuba's second largest crop is tobacco. Toward the center of the island the broad-leaved plants cover acre on acre. Freight cars piled high with bundles of tobacco leaves chug into Havana to supply the hundreds of men and women who roll the cigars for which Cuba is famous.

These are all products from agricultural Cuba. But now the island's mineral wealth is of particular interest to us. Her deposits of manganese and chromium are necessary in making steel. Last year we bought all of the iron ore she exported. Copper, antimony, mercury, and many other minerals are produced in smaller amounts. Some day the island's coal and asphalt beds will be of world importance.

Cuba is fortunate in having a good network of roads stretching out over the island. The finest of all is the

700-mile Central Highway. A seventy-carat diamond sunk in the floor of the Capitol in Havana marks its zero mile point.

The narrow, crowded streets of old Havana lead away from the waterfront. Tiny shops full of jumbled wares line the crooked streets. The walls are old and thick and scarred. Near the center of the city buildings more than four centuries old border quiet little squares. The grilled iron balconies overhang cobbled streets and a half open door lets you peek at a flower-filled patio inside. Havana's famous old cathedral stands away from the busy streets of the city facing such a square. The walls are old and musty, but inside there are beautiful arches enclosing tiny chapels and richly colored paintings. The Convent of Santa Clara, now occupied by a department of the government, is one of the oldest of old Havana's buildings. Inside in its patio are two tiny buildings. One of them is called the "Sailor's House." The tale runs that once a sailor lived in this tiny house and because he disapproved of his daughter's beau, he kept her locked in the house until she died.

CUBAN SUGAR MILL

Cubans will tell you that their Capitol Building is the most beautiful in the world, and cost twenty-five million dollars to build. It faces on Havana's most photographed street, The Prado, which joins with the lovely Malecón Drive running along the seawall and out past the statue of Martí, national hero of Cuba.

It was Martí who from boyhood always kept before

SUGAR CANE CUT AS "SEED" FOR PLANTING

him the dream of a free Cuba. Last of the Spanish colonies to become independent of the mother country, Cuba won her independence in 1898.

HAITI

Although Cuba is less a stranger than most of the American Republics, few of us know the two little nations that share the island of Hispaniola next door. Haiti's three million people are crowded 275 to the square mile on the western third of the island. The Dominican Republic spreads over the other two-thirds. The island is a jumble of hills and mountains with rich valleys between. A steep mountain range runs like a sharp backbone the length of the island. The two nations have much the same climate, raise many of the same crops, have many of the same problems. But they also have differences which sharply divide them. Haiti is a Negro republic. Its coffee plantations that stretch out over the end of the island are owned and worked by Negroes. The little farms that dot the fertile valleys belong to Negroes and so do the large, white stone houses that stand in its cities. High on the mountain looking over the port stands the gigantic *Citadelle Laferrière* built by Henri Christophe who made himself King of Haiti, and was one of the richest kings on earth. The great fort has been called the eighth wonder of the world. Even women and children trudged up the hill with loads of sand and stone to build it. And always the stern commands of the king rang out, to hurry the work lest the enemy arrive and find them unprepared. It was in this fort that the king hoped to find refuge if the French arrived to try to retake the little country.

For France was once the mother country of Haiti, the one French-speaking nation among the American Republics. The story dips back into the past, to the days when pirates and buccaneers sailed the Caribbean. French pirates with their stronghold on the little island of Tortuga, near Hispaniola, became bolder. Finally they settled here and there on the western end. Spain and France kept up a constant bickering over these settlements until they signed the treaty which gave France possession of what had already been taken. But the days that followed contrasted sharply with the first settlements of pirates. Again sugar cane played an important part in the life of one of our near neighbors. In 1594 a missionary from the Canary Islands brought shoots of sugar cane to the island, and soon great plantations spread over the fertile, damp soil.

It is hard to imagine a time when the sugar bowl wasn't on every table. But in Europe in the sixteenth

Photo by Ewing Galloway, N. Y.

NATIVE HUT IN HAITI

century sugar was very scarce and very expensive. Only the very wealthy could afford it, and honey was used instead for sweetening. As the island's cane plantations increased the price of sugar dropped enough so that more people could buy and Europe snatched up all that the islands had to sell. Even then it was several dollars a pound. The plantation owners became enormously wealthy. Lords and ladies came from France to live in this prosperous colony. Dressed in their clothes from Paris and Madrid they were a splendid sight as they drove through the streets. Their coaches were upholstered in the finest tapestries and the harnesses of their horses were mounted with silver. It is said that even kings and queens in Europe were jealous of the wealthy sugar planters.

It was to work the fields that the first Negroes were brought as slaves from Africa to the island, and from here they spread over into Cuba. Hard labor, warfare, and disease had wiped out most of the Indians found there when the Spaniards settled the islands. It is true that a large part of Cuba's population is Negro or Negro and white mixed, and the same is true of the Dominican Republic. But Haiti is almost entirely black. For a long time white people could not even own property there. And when the country gained its independence from France—the first of the Latin American nations to become independent—a Negro headed the government. But when the long struggle for independence was over, the cane fields were laid waste, the great houses burned, and the country was unbelievably poor. Her people had proved themselves brave warriors, but they were untrained in ruling a country. Disorder was everywhere. The money they borrowed from foreign countries they could not repay. Threatened by the countries they owed and in a turmoil within, affairs reached a climax when their president was murdered. The United States took a hand in the country's affairs and sent in Marines to keep order and a customs collector and a financial adviser to help them get their affairs in better shape.

Slowly but steadily the little island is working out its problems. A few years ago it asked the United States for assistance—neither military nor financial this time. They asked for an expert in agriculture who would advise them on the crops they should plant and the best method of cultivating them. The invitation was for a three months' stay—which stretched to twenty months. New crops and increased production of old ones will help this little country climb back to the position it once held as a prosperous nation.

GATHERING DATES ON DOMINICAN PLANTATION

DOMINICAN REPUBLIC

The Dominican Republic is proud of the fact that its capital is the oldest permanent European settlement in the New World. The "House of the Admiral," built by Columbus's son Diego in 1514, still stands today. Not far from it is the church of San Nicolás, oldest Christian church in America. Here on this nation's shores the Columbus Memorial to be built by the American nations will stand. In the form of a lighthouse, the memorial will be the resting place for Columbus's bones.

The Dominican Republic has struggled with many of the same problems that have troubled Haiti. From a prosperous country, famous for the wealth and social life of its capital, it went through troublous days both before and after it became independent from Spain. Once for two years it was taken over by Haiti. Another time it even asked the United States to take it over as a colony. Its story repeats much of Haiti's— debt, disorder, and the arrival of American Marines. But from a poverty-stricken, disorganized nation the

CORN HUNG OUT TO DRY, SANTO DOMINGO

Dominican Republic is quickly becoming a progressive country. Good roads spread out through the country and lead to the ports where its principal crops—sugar, cacao, cotton, and tobacco are shipped to other countries. But the Dominican Republic does not have a large population. It has rich, fertile land where many different crops will grow, but it lacks people to culti-

31

vate its fields and develop these crops.

The country's plan to settle refugees there may help solve their agricultural problem. Early in 1940 the Dominican Republic offered to take in 100,000 refugees from Europe. Some 26,000 acres were set aside for the settlement. The first group to arrive were thirty-seven refugees from Italy. If the experiment is a success, as it shows promise of being, it will not only provide new homes and a new life for many homeless people, but will benefit the country as well.

These three little nations were the first glimpse Columbus had of America on his first voyage. For many years they were the center of the Spanish empire in the New World. From here Balboa and Pizarro turned southward and Cortes and his adventurous band moved into Mexico. From here De Soto pushed northward to discover the Mississippi River and was buried in its waters. The grim, gray stone forts that guard the entrance to their ports are reminders of the days when their riches made them the envy of every other nation. Here ships loaded with the gold and silver and jewels from the mainland of the Americas met the galleons that transferred the riches to Spain. Soon other ships, flying pirate flags, their decks swarming with bold fierce-faced men, rings in their ears and cutlasses in their hands, slipped up near the islands and swooped down on the richly laden vessels. Seldom a month passed without thrilling sea battles fought off the shores.

Today the pirate ships and the Spanish galleons have gone from the Caribbean, but still the forts stand guard over a rich prize. Lying in the pathway leading to the Panama Canal, and not far from our own shores, these three American nations are important to us because of their position.

3

SOUTH OF THE BORDER—MEXICO

RED HILL (*"Cuesta Colorada"*) is the name on the sign marking a curve on the highway this side of Mexico City. Over the edge of the road the precipice drops down to a deep valley nestling between the mountains and the high plateau. The scene below is not unlike a child's toy village. Red earth outlines the small plots of corn and beans and vegetable gardens and here and there shows bright between the rows. A small stream winds in and out, as though uncertain of its way, across the valley. The motionless waters of a tiny pond reflect the scene around it. Blue smoke rises from thatched houses that dot the valley. Dogs and children play near the doorways as their parents work in the fields. Speeding motorists, bent on reaching Mexico City by nightfall,

CATHEDRAL IN MEXICO CITY

note the sign without slackening their speed and do not see the valley below. Yet this little valley, but a dot compared with the enormous, sprawling Mexico, is part of a program to settle the Indian on the land. It is an answer to the cry that has re-echoed through

Mexico since the revolution of 1910—"Land for those who work it." It is the thing that is happening in Mexico that sets that country apart from the other American Republics.

The King of Spain rewarded the conquerors of Mexico not only with enormous tracts of land, but with Indians to cultivate it. More colonists came, more land was settled, and more Indians were needed to work. As the land was divided among colonists, plots were set aside for the Indian villages. Here the Indians lived in their little huts and farmed the lands surrounding the villages. In many ways the great estates of Mexico with their Indian laborers were like our own southern plantations worked by Negroes. After Mexico's independence, the country, although rich in resources, had little money with which to develop them. Business men and governments of foreign countries were invited to invest their money in Mexico to work the mines, drill the oil wells, build railways and power plants. And companies who surveyed Mexico's land were given huge slices of it in payment. Sometimes they received almost a third of the land they had sur-

MOUNT POPOCATEPETL IN MEXICO IS 17,520 FEET HIGH AND IS SNOW-
CROWNED ALL YEAR ROUND

veyed. But although Mexico is a large country, a
fourth as large as the United States, it could not go on
handing out land to everyone. So when they ran short
they took more and more of the Indian village land
away from the Indians. The Indians, left without land,
were forced to work on the *haciendas,* or plantations.

37

Sometimes they were given little patches of land to work as their own in exchange for their labor. Sometimes they worked as day laborers. Their hours were long and the pay poor and they were practically slaves. Some of the Indians refused to work on the *haciendas*. Taking their household goods—a few clay pots, their straw mats, their chickens, perhaps a goat and burro, always a dog—they pushed farther up into the mountains. Today their farms are tilted high on rocky slopes so steep that no oxen could pull a plow there. The Indians plant the corn with a sharpened stick and cultivate it with a hoe.

Then a revolution against the large land owners and this way of life broke out. For ten years it raged. Villages were burned, railroads ruined, crops destroyed, the government's treasury left without money, and a million people had been killed.

But a section in the new constitution, written after the revolution, promised the return of the village land to the peasants. Under the constitution the lands which were not under cultivation were also to be divided among the landless.

But the work of distributing the land went slowly. Each President shirked the task of taking land from the big landholders to give to the Indians. At times it looked as if that section of the constitution were forgotten. But the Indian did not forget the promise. And, finally, when he began to seize land for himself, the government began to cut down the big *haciendas* in order to distribute land among the peasants. Each year more and more land was taken from the huge estates and more and more landless Indians were settled on the soil which had once belonged to their forefathers.

But dividing the land did not solve all of the problems of Mexico. The land alone had little value if there was no money to buy seeds, no machinery with which to till the soil, and no one to instruct the laborer what to plant and how to plant it. Crops were poor and there was a scarcity of food. People criticized the program and the Indians.

Meanwhile a new slogan was heard: "Mexico for the Mexicans." It expressed the grievance of the laborers against the industries held by foreign companies.

The investors found rich mines, good oil, and fertile fields. The labor was cheap and the profits large. A great share of the money they made was sent out of the country. The people began to realize that money kept in the country would build more factories, put more people to work. And like the laborers on the land, they demanded a share of the industries and a voice in running them. And like the land problem, the problem of the industries is beginning to be settled by giving the laborers a share in the industries and a hand in the management. Some progress has been made. The worst trouble came when the Mexican government seized the oil wells held by British and American companies. In long-drawn-out conferences the Mexican government and the representatives of the companies talked over the amount of money to be paid for the oil holdings. They have not yet been able to agree. The land division and the oil dispute are difficult problems to solve. Like all disputes, it has two sides, neither of which may be all wrong or all right.

What is this great country of Mexico like? The crumpled piece of paper again answers the question. It

MEXICAN BOY WITH KID

has the same great mountains, high plateaus, and lowlands found almost everywhere in Latin America. A great highland plateau sweeps through the center of Mexico, vast as our own Middle Western plains. Here are the great corn and wheat fields, the cattle ranches, and here lives the majority of the population. It is on this plateau with its agreeable climate that Mexico City, the capital, is located.

In northwestern Mexico warm sunlit days follow one after another for months on end and rain seldom if ever falls. But the land is fertile, and where irrigation ditches carry water to the thirsty acres, large cotton plantations are covering the desert. Most of them are worked as co-operatives and in their midst little communities with schools, hospitals, and stores have been built.

Across the country, in the warm lowlands of southeastern Mexico, thousands of acres bristle with the tall, stiff spikes of the henequén plant. Binder twine is made from the fibers and most of Mexico's crop is used in the harvest fields of the United States and Canada. Most of the great henequén plantations have been cut up into smaller farms or worked as co-operatives. Smaller plots are being planted to a variety of crops to furnish a better rounded diet for the laborers.

The tropical climate of Mexico's southern coast is well fitted to grow bananas. Within the last ten years plantations have increased so fast that Mexico is moving toward the head of the list of banana-exporting countries.

Deep within the mountain ranges that edge the plateau on east and west, Mexico's rich mineral wealth is buried. There are the silver mines which produce more silver than any in the world. Huge fortunes were built from these mines in colonial days and fantastic tales of how it was spent are still repeated in Mexico. They tell the story of a man who, when his daughter was married, paved the path of the wedding procession with silver slabs. Rich ornaments of gold and silver still left in churches and public buildings in Mexico today are proof of many other stories. Gold, lead, zinc, and copper, together with silver, top the list of the country's principal minerals. But although these five are the most important in value, Mexico has many

Photo by Ewing Galloway, N. Y.

LOADS OF HENEQUÉN SPIKES ON THE WAY TO THE MILL AT GRANADA,
MEXICO. THESE SPIKES PRODUCE FIBER USED IN MAKING ROPE

other minerals not mined in such quantity. Today they
are of increasing importance because many of them are
absolutely necessary to modern industry. Antimony,
graphite, mercury, tin, and many others will be mentioned again and more fully in another chapter of this
book.

But Mexico's wealth does not rest alone in its agri-

BALES OF FIBER PRODUCED FROM THE HENEQUÉN PLANT IN MEXICO

culture and metals. In addition to valuable minerals, great petroleum fields along the east coast and southeastern coast place Mexico seventh among oil-producing countries in the world.

Nature, so generous to Mexico in natural resources, is stingy in water supply. In northern Mexico for one hundred and fifty miles between the International

Bridge and Monterrey there is little but desert and tall, prickly cactus, and in the spring mile upon mile of yellow mesquite. Lonely adobe houses stand here and there near the highway. Bright flowers blossom in the windows and children play in the open doorways. Speeding cars crowd the jogging burro from the highway and blind him with dust as they rush on toward the tall buildings and smoking chimneys of Monterrey, "the Pittsburgh of Mexico." It is a busy city of foundries and factories and mills, a mixture of Mexican and American, where almost everyone can make himself understood in English and—better still— where almost everyone can understand our Spanish!

Mexico City, León, Puebla, and Guadalajara complete the list of Mexico's industrial cities. A permanent exhibit in a corner of the Palace of Fine Arts in Mexico City shows the products of factory, foundry, shop, and mill. There is lovely glassware and beautiful pottery. There are bolts on bolts of evenly woven cotton and woolen cloth for which the country is fast becoming important. Near by are row on row of shoes made from leather tanned and dyed in the country.

CACTUS FENCE NEAR MEXICO CITY

There are shelves filled with brushes and combs, inks and paints, paper and rubber goods. Fruits and vegetables preserved in Mexican canning factories and fish caught in its waters fill several shelves. Samples of mineral wealth—silver, gold, zinc, petroleum, iron, mercury, and many others—fill a glass case. Mexico's industries began on a small scale to supply her own needs and take the place of expensive imported goods.

But Mexico is not alone a country of fertile fields, of rich mines and growing industries. It is a country whose history was old when Columbus discovered the New World. It is a land where the old rubs elbows with the new. Built in a valley in the shadow of snow-covered Popocatepetl and Ixtaccihuatl, Mexico City, twice as large as our own capital, is many years older. Deeply carved stone churches and ornate public buildings of colonial days share the same block with streamlined modern buildings. Automobiles of the latest models, caught in the traffic jam of a busy street, pause beside an old lady selling violets before a century-old chapel. The barefooted Indian in *sombrero* and *poncho* pauses before the shop window filled with the latest electric gadgets. Within a half hour's ride from the city's busy streets is ancient Mexico, three thousand years old, some people believe. Towering over the little village near by is the Pyramid of the Sun. Its base spreads over eleven acres and it rises two hundred and ten feet high. The path with the uninviting name "Road of the Dead" leads past the unfinished Temple

FIRE IN A MEXICAN OIL FIELD

SILVER MINE AT PACHUCA, MEXICO

of Quetzalcoatl to the Pyramid of the Moon. The plumed serpent's heads carved deeply into the stone of the temple still stare at the passer-by. The slabs of stone, fitted so carefully by the Toltec builders that they hold as though cemented, still stand firm today. Not far away and in a dozen scattered spots throughout Mexico men trained to read history by carved stones, the shape of a pottery jar, the designs on gold and silver jewelry, patiently work to piece together the nation's story.

Thousands of Indians throughout Mexico still pattern their days by those of their forefathers. The fisherman in his dug-out on Lake Patzcuaro still uses the lacelike butterfly nets. The potter at Mitla, City of the Dead, still molds the same black water jars. Toluca's basket maker and the weaver in Texcoco weave in the bright designs learned from their parents. As the Indian takes his place in the new Mexico, gradually his days will follow new patterns. In exchange for better food, a more comfortable house, schools for his children, and hospitals for his sick, the Indian will give some of the rich culture of his forefathers. Already modern Mexico is learning the value of co-operation from the Indian.

4

IN MIDDLE AMERICA—NICARAGUA, GUATEMALA, COSTA RICA

NAME the five countries of Central America." This was the question put to the dean of a state university in a recent radio quiz. For a few moments there was deep silence. Then the sympathetic announcer began to throw out helpful hints. But the gong sounded before even one country was named.

Perhaps few of the dean's audience could have helped him out. When they are thought of at all—and usually they aren't—it is as a part of South America. Not rich in developed minerals nor densely populated, this group of little countries lying just below Mexico is important because of its position. Bordering on the Panama Canal and containing the route over which the United States has the right to dig a second canal, what happens there is anxiously watched by this country. The whole of Central America is about the size of California. But it is a small edition of Latin America as a whole. It has the many different climates, the lofty peaks of rugged mountain ranges, and the coastal lowlands. There are the same groups of people: the White European, the darker *mestizo* (the person with white and Indian blood), the pure Indian, the Negro and the mulatto (Negro and white), sometimes a mixture of Indian and Negro.

Here, too, within this small territory, are the contrasts that set the twenty American Republics apart as separate nations, each with its own personality. Guatemala, Honduras, and Nicaragua all have a large Indian and *mestizo* population. But the Indians aren't alike! They don't speak the same language, wear the same clothes, or celebrate the same holidays. And holidays are as important to an Indian as they are to a schoolboy. Salvador is a small, bustling country about the size of the Netherlands. It has few Indians, but so many other people that they are crowded closely together. Their busy workshops and mills and closely set villages contrast sharply with lonely stretches in the interior of Guatemala, Honduras, and Nicaragua where the few people take things at a slower pace.

Costa Rica is still different from all the other four. Its people are almost all white and most of them live on small plantations. It is an orderly little country, well deserving the good reputation it enjoys not only in Central America but in the Western Hemisphere.

These contrasts are part of the stumbling block in the path of each Central American president who ever dreamed of a Central American Union. It is the answer to people little acquainted with these five countries, who ask, "Why don't these little, weak countries unite and make one big strong country?" It isn't a new idea and it was tried back in 1821. The Confederation lasted nineteen years, but finally broke up into the five separate nations as they are today. Let's take a closer look at three of them: Nicaragua, Guatemala, and Costa Rica.

CHICLE HUNTER IN GUATEMALA. THE SAP FLOWS DOWN GASHES CUT IN
THE TREE

NICARAGUA

Newspaper headlines often mention Nicaragua. Sometimes they herald the arrival of its President on a neighborly visit. Oftener they have something to say about a Nicaraguan canal, and you find it in the inside section. Twenty-six years ago the Nicaragua Canal was front page news. That was when the United States paid three million dollars for the right to build a canal across Nicaragua. And ever since that day that country's affairs have been of particular interest to us.

It wasn't a new idea, even then. Several centuries before, a Dutchman reporting on possible canal sites in the New World mentioned Nicaragua as one. But nothing came of the suggestion. Years later gold was discovered in California. It was a long trek in covered wagons from the East to the West. Eagerly the prospectors scanned maps to find an easier route to the gold fields. Then Commodore Vanderbilt, a New Yorker with a love of adventure and the money to satisfy it, hit upon a great idea. Searching the map for

56

possible ways to reach California he noticed in Nicaragua a very large lake, about a third as large as Lake Erie. Two rivers, one on the east and one near the west coast, almost joined the lake. Sailing over the calm waters of river and lake would be quicker and more comfortable than the long trek over rough, Indian-infested country, he thought.

Shortly thereafter, steamers leaving from New York and New Orleans carried eager crowds to Greytown on Nicaragua's eastern coast. The travelers continued up the San Juan del Norte (St. John of the North) river, then landed to make their way around the swift rapids. Next the vast, blue waters of Lake Nicaragua carried them ninety-two miles nearer their tempting goal and brought them to another river, San Juan del Sur (St. John of the South). The journey by river ended and they had yet a twelve mile overland journey to bring them to the Pacific Ocean. For this part of the journey Mr. Vanderbilt had provided in grand style. A hard-surfaced road joined the river with the coast. Bright blue carriages drawn by high-spirited horses whisked the passengers over the smooth highway. Always traveling in groups of twenty-five carriages, they carried a daring crowd looking forward to great wealth and easy living. The fare was $300 for the entire trip and as many as 25,000 people made the journey each year. After the gold rush there was little travel and later, with fighting and disorder in the country, the trips were discontinued.

But the question of a canal bobbed up in the news now and then. Finally, in 1914, the United States decided the question of *who* would build it when she bought the right from Nicaragua. *When* has never been decided. If it should be built at all is a question on which people have long, heated arguments. Those not in favor say that we have the Panama Canal and don't need another; that should an enemy destroy the Panama Canal they would also destroy the Nicaragua, not far away. Those who say we should build the Nicaragua Canal deny that if the one at Panama were destroyed it would necessarily follow that the one in Nicaragua would also be put out of commission. They argue that by using Lake Nicaragua much of the work is already done. These are only some of the arguments

CHICLE SAP FLOWING INTO BAG

in this long-drawn-out debate.

The United States figured in another chapter of Nicaragua's story. Indirectly this came about over the location of the country's capital. The Conservatives in the staid old city of Granada and the Liberals of more progressive León each saw their city as the perfect nation's capital. The argument became more heated and finally broke into open warfare. News of the trouble reached William Walker, a slight, tow-headed, freckle-faced Tennessean. With fifty-eight equally adventurous countrymen he arrived in Nicaragua and the battle began. The real—and rumored—episodes of Walker would fill a book. But not even a Horatio Alger hero ever rivaled Walker's achievement in having himself elected President of Nicaragua. No American citizen had ever before headed a foreign government. None has since. He occupied his high position only for a year, when he was deposed and later shot. And after all of the trouble neither León nor Granada won, for the capital was moved to Managua.

Meanwhile affairs in Nicaragua did not improve

Peace lasting from a few months to a few years always ended in revolution. United States companies with investments in Nicaragua were anxious to have order restored. Many of them even suggested that our government do something about it. At last the Conservative President of the country called on the United States and found this country not unwilling to take an active part in the affairs of its neighbor. In 1910 the first United States Marines arrived in Nicaragua. Off and on for the next twenty-two years the Leathernecks were familiar figures in the ports and throughout the country. And as time went on, different jobs came up for them to do. They supervised elections and chased bandits. In 1930 when an earthquake in less than two minutes tumbled Managua, Nicaragua's capital, to the ground, the Marines helped in the grim task of restoring order out of chaos. Nevertheless many Nicaraguans were annoyed at the idea of having the Marines there. They were a constant reminder that foreigners were helping run their country. Whether or not they needed help in managing their affairs was beside the point. They felt about the Marines as most

61

of us feel about medicine. It may help us but it's hard to take. Nor were the Nicaraguans alone in their feeling. The other four Central American countries, in particular, anxiously watching affairs in Nicaragua, knew that the same things could happen in their own countries, too. Costa Rica was especially critical of the United States. Even many people in this country objected to the Marine occupation. Finally, on New Year's Day 1933 the last boatful of cheering Marines steamed out of Corinto.

When the Spaniards came to Nicaragua they found roving, not highly civilized Indians. Spaniard and Indian intermarried and today more than half of the people are *mestizos*. A fourth of the people, mostly in the cities, are of pure Spanish blood. Perhaps ten per cent are pure Indian and the rest are Negroes living along the east coast.

Dense forests of mahogany, cedar, and many other rich cabinet woods cover the eastern lowlands. Bananas are a big crop in the low, damp parts of the country, and in the cool highlands coffee and cacao are among the biggest crops. Large herds of cattle roaming the

Photo by Ewing Galloway, N. Y.

CHICLE SAP IS BOILED UNTIL IT STIFFENS LIKE TAFFY

grasslands furnish thousands of pounds of hides and skins for export. Many years of constant disorder gave Nicaragua little opportunity until recently to improve its land, develop its minerals, and build industries.

63

GUATEMALA

Four centuries ago Pedro Alvarado, a tall, blond-haired, blue-eyed man, galloped into Guatemala at the head of a troop of Spanish soldiers, conquered the Indians, and claimed the country for Spain. Recently another army has invaded Guatemala. By land, sea, and air, artists and photographers have arrived to catch on canvas and screen the life and color of this fascinating country.

Their pictures show many contrasts: Indian Guatemala of the highland villages with their many-colored costumes and extreme styles; colonial Guatemala of Antigua with its thick old walls, flower-filled gardens, and restful parks; and modern, progressive Guatemala of the beautiful well-kept capital, Guatemala City.

Within a country the size of Ohio is a Guatemala old when Columbus accidentally discovered America and as new as its spotlessly clean, beautiful airport. In its capital, a modern city of 165,000 people, there is always a mingling of old and new. The plane that puts you down at the airport is of the latest model. But the

PACK PEDDLER IN GUATEMALA

little Indian girl who greets you with the basket of fragrant gardenias is dressed in the costume which her tribe has worn for centuries. There is a reminder of Indian Guatemala in the murals that decorate the interior of the building where you are served cups of delicious hot coffee, for which Guatemala is famous.

Guatemala City is like any number of other cities

in the things that make up a city: modern shops, wide paved streets, well-kept parks, and a remarkably clean market. But few cities are so fortunate in their location. Lofty mountains encircle it and the volcanoes of *Agua* and *Fuego* (Water and Fire) rise many thousand feet to stand guard over the valley. Sometimes their cones show sharp and clear to the very top. More often a thin gray mist floats restlessly from cone to base like a chiffon veil.

But Antigua, the old capital of Guatemala, is a reminder of a time when the volcanoes were not so peaceful as they have been lately. Built almost four hundred years ago, it was one of the most beautiful cities between Mexico City and Peru. All roads led to it, and over them were carried the beautiful and costly goods which arrived on every ship from Spain. It had great public buildings, many beautiful churches decorated by famous artists, fine schools in which some of Europe's most learned scholars taught. When only Indians lived where New York and Washington and Chicago now stand, ladies gowned in stiff brocades and gentlemen in velvet and plumes drove through the streets of Antigua in expensive coaches. To add to its glory, it was given a very long and very grand name— "Most Noble and Loyal City of St. James of the Knights of Guatemala."

Then one afternoon the sky darkened, the earth shook, and the side of *Agua* gave way with a terrific roar. The water that had filled its craters poured down the mountainside bringing rocks and mud that filled the valley. The people who rushed into the streets were swept into the current. Those who stayed inside were struck down by falling walls and tumbling roofs. The city was rebuilt, but later in 1773 a terrible earthquake ruined most of it again and the capital was moved to its present location. Today Antigua is a quiet, peaceful town. Many of the buildings were repaired and restored. But everywhere there are crumbling walls almost overgrown with vines and flowers. Its beautifully arched buildings, wooden-grilled windows, and carved doors hint at its former beauty. Its churches are among the most beautiful in the Americas.

The building where the Central American Federation held its meetings almost a century ago escaped unharmed and is now a hotel. The thick walls, that once re-echoed the fiery speeches of delegates, muffle the voices of guests demanding hot water or an extra blanket. For when the sun drops behind the volcanoes the air is sharp. In one of Antigua's quiet streets stands the house where Bernal Diaz del Castillo, a fiery captain who marched with Cortes, wrote his "true account of the conquest of Mexico." In the stillness that blankets the old city it is easy to believe the wide-eyed servants who tell weird stories of the ghosts who walk in the moonlight, of old Brother Peter who goes through the streets ringing his bell to warn all evil-doers to mend their ways.

Guatemala has 3,001,750 people, more than any other country of Central America. Almost three-fourths of them are pure or part Indian. The Guatemalan Indian keeps to himself as much as possible. High in the mountains or nestling in the valleys between they have built their villages. Here they weave the bright birds, strange animals, and spindly-legged people into the colorful textiles for which they are famous. Before his house in the warm sunshine the

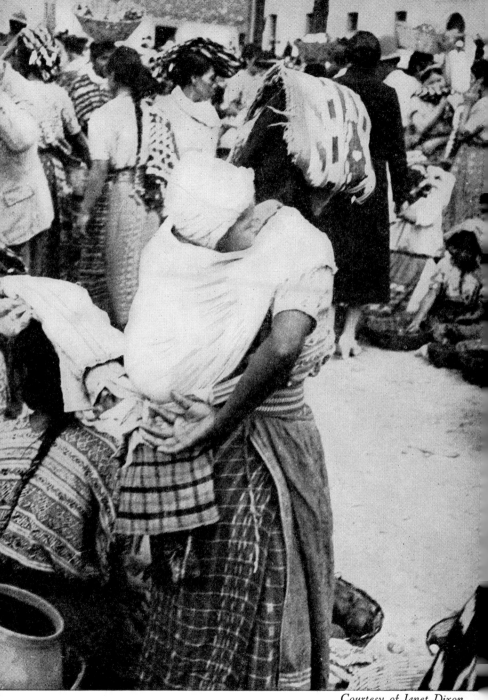

Courtesy of Janet Dixon

MARKET IN SAN PEDRO, GUATEMALA

Indian fashions pottery on ancient molds and decorates them with strange figures. Tilling the soil that he loves, gathering the harvest, and celebrating his fiestas he follows the century-old customs of his people. In the village near by he exchanges what he makes for a few simple things he does not produce.

Once or twice a week the family rises in the black hours before dawn and prepares for the long walk to the city market. The mother wraps a striped shawl around her shoulders, fastens it securely at the waist, and tucks a tiny dark-eyed baby inside. Then she swings an enormous basket filled with hundreds of eggs, vegetables, fruits, or meat atop her head. Sometimes live chickens peek over the edge of the basket, like birds trimming a cartwheel hat. In a small basket she carries food for the family—flabby tortillas, red chilis, chocolate or coffee, black beans, and fruit. The father lifts a heavy frame filled with pottery, textiles, or grain to his back and fixes the tumpline around his forehead. Bending low beneath the weight he takes the long trail to the city. Boys and girls dressed exactly like the father and mother trot beside them. Often

Photo by Ewing Galloway, N. Y.

GUATEMALA CITY, GUATEMALA

they carry smaller baskets or urge three or four squeal-
ing pigs along the road.

Like sturdy little pack ponies, they jog along with
their peculiar trot quickly covering the long distance
between home and market. The early morning sun rising over the mountains picks out the bright colors of
their garments as they descend the long trail, like a

71

string of gay, many-colored beads. Sandaled feet slap the pavement as they enter the city and pass swiftly to the great central market.

With their wares arranged in stalls or piled in little mounds around them on the ground, they chat with their neighbors and relax after the long trek. Soon customers arrive. The mistress and servants from the city homes come to buy food and flowers, pottery bowls, or a basket or two. Lively bargaining and many gestures accompany each purchase.

When the last articles are sold, the Indian women go through the market making their simple purchases —a few spices, spools of bright thread, a bag of sugar, or a piece of soap. And when the shadows lengthen across the marketplace, the Indians gather the children together and once more turn back to the lonely upland trails.

But not all of the Indians have their own patch of soil to till. Guatemala is an agricultural country. There are coffee plantations—*fincas*—of thousands of acres to cultivate. Chicle must be gathered from the *zapote* trees in the hot Petén jungle to keep the gum-chewing public well stocked. Near the coast mile upon mile of bananas need careful attention. For all of these laborers are needed: Indians for the highland plantations, mostly Negroes in the banana lands of the lowlands. Often the coffee planter used to stride into the Indian villages and demand laborers for his plantation. The wages were low and the Indians spent them in advance at the plantation store. When the harvest was over his wages were gone and he was held on the plantation to work off the debt. But instead of growing less it increased and the Indian became little more than a slave, held over season after season but homesick for his highland village.

Four years ago a new law was passed forbidding this system of forced labor. All the Indian's debts were canceled and he started fresh as his own master. Many of them stayed on where they had worked, as our southern slaves did after slavery was abolished here. Another new law is supposed to help the Indian become self-supporting. If he has produced twenty armfuls of corn, beans, wheat, or whatever crop he planted, he must work another hundred days a year for wages. If he has no land he must work one hundred and fifty days. But he may work as many days at a time as he chooses and for whomever he chooses. On the large plantations where many Indian families work the year round, the owner must provide a school for the children.

A country with so many different climates—the hot lowland, the cool plateaus, and cold highlands—can produce a variety of products. Since colonial days, however, Guatemala's wealth has depended on a few crops. Gradually more smaller crops are being planted for food. Still other crops are being developed. A few industries are springing up, but Guatemala's future like its past is likely to depend on agriculture. Returns from the tourist trade will help out the budget in this "land of eternal springtime."

COSTA RICA

"We have two armies," Costa Ricans say. "The military with nine barracks and 246 soldiers, and the scholastic with 475 schools, 1,902 teachers and 51,500 pupils." Teachers rather than soldiers have played the most important part in this country's development.

Farthest south of the Central Americas, Costa Rica is a trim little country the size of West Virginia. It has few people, less than the population of Washington, D. C. Eighty per cent are white and live on the high plateau where their Spanish ancestors first settled in the sixteenth century. Few have the darker skin of the white and Indian mixed. Fewer still are pure Indian. Neither white nor Indian has mixed with the Negroes brought in to cultivate the banana lands near the coast.

San José, the capital, ringed about with mountain peaks, has a well-kept look and an unhurried manner. There is less of the noise, glare, and bustle of the up-to-date business city and more of the peace and quiet of a village. But its modern shops, broad streets, schools, and hospitals prove it a progressive little city. In the later afternoon people promenade in the central park. According to the old Spanish custom, the men go around the park one way and the ladies the other. Youths lounge against grilled windows to chat with beautiful *señoritas* inside. Costa Ricans say,

LOADING BANANAS IN COSTA RICA

"And perilous spots are the window places, for mothers whose daughters have pretty faces!" The early evening quiet is broken by the siren warning lagging movie fans that the picture is about to begin.

But Costa Rica has not always presented such a pleasant picture. Time was when its name—"rich coast"—mocked the discouraged colonists and was

76

Photo by Ewing Galloway, N. Y.

HAULING BANANAS TO THE RAILROAD IN COSTA RICA

spoken in scorn by the neighboring countries. The Indians who stared with wonder at Columbus as he touched shore here on his fourth voyage wore golden ornaments. And the little band set ashore with Bartholomew Columbus to colonize had high hopes of becoming very rich. But they soon found that the Indians wore the gold not because there was so much but

77

because it was so rare. Nor did the *conquistadores* who followed on the heels of Columbus waste time in a country that had no ready wealth. But some of the hardiest colonists stayed on. They knew that riches, if any, would be gained by hard work. Unlike the Indians in Mexico and Guatemala, the Costa Rican Indians farmed only enough to supply part of their food. They were more like our own North American tribes, a roving lot who hunted and fished as they moved onward. When the colonists tried to put them to work, they pushed farther into the jungle or higher into the mountains.

But poor as the little country was in its early days, it was fortunate in its colonists. Peaceful, hard-working farmers of northern Spain, capable leaders, and proudly patriotic Basques crowded into the boats setting sail for this part of the New World. Like our own Pilgrims, they worked their land side by side. Together they joined forces to fight off the Mosquito Indians of Nicaragua and the English and Dutch pirates who swooped down on the east coast. The democratic spirit developed then still remains.

With the help of the government, the people planted coffee on the cool highlands. The climate was particularly well suited to its growth and coffee drinkers in London, where most of it was sold, were glad to get this good brand. When the Costa Rican railroad was finished more than seventy years ago, the builder looked around for freight to haul. Bananas grow fast and bear fruit within a year after planting. So shoots were brought from Panama and stuck in the rich, damp soil of the coastal lowlands. The shoots were the beginning of the great plantations stretching over hundreds of acres today. From the first year's harvest 250 stems were sent to New Orleans. People bought the strange new fruit, then wondered how to eat it. Those who ate the skin and threw the pulp away didn't think much of it. But those who reversed the order rushed to buy more and the banana was on its way to its present popularity.

Banana and coffee plantations need constant care. The landlord with coffee to weed and bananas to cut had little time for fighting. Most of the people had their own plots of land. There were few landless who might gain much or lose little through a revolution. Today the greater part of Costa Rica's land owners still live on the land and superintend its cultivation.

With little mixture of race and language, Costa Rica has not been faced with many of the problems which other American nations are still struggling to solve. Costa Rica has kept close ties with Europe. Until the war, most of her trade was with those countries, and when the youth of Costa Rica looked beyond his country for education it was in the schools of France or England or Spain that he usually enrolled. But during recent years Costa Rica has showed her willingness to co-operate with her neighbor nations.

5

AT THE CROSSROADS—PANAMA

PANAMA, "place abounding in fish," the Indians called the neck of land connecting Central and South America. Here in the streams and in the forest-covered mountains and thick jungles they hunted their food. Here they lived in their villages of grass huts. Poking in and out of the ports from Costa Rica to South America, Columbus touched shore there on his fourth voyage. But the little village of fishermen was not an impressive sight to one searching for the riches of India. There was no indication that one day this small country would occupy such an important place in the world.

Today this little crescent-shaped country contains the Canal Zone—five hundred square miles of land more anxiously guarded than any part of our territory. Forming a five-mile border on each side of the Panama Canal, it has been called the "keystone of our defense," for the safety of the hemisphere depends upon it.

Colon's busy shops and 30,000 people are crowded between the Atlantic docks and New Cristobal, the American section of the city. There is little about Colon and Panama City to remind one of the fishing villages which Columbus saw more than four centuries ago. Panama City, with almost 83,000 people, stands on the Pacific side facing westward. In its Central Plaza filled with oleander and palm and bright tropical flowers, the Declaration of Independence was signed. Its narrow, crooked streets are lined with shops filled with wares from the ends of the earth. Silk mandarin coats sway gently in the doorway of Chinese stores. Inside cases are crowded with jade and carved ivory and delicate porcelain. Brilliant silks and linens and embroidered shawls are tossed carelessly over bamboo furniture and lacquer chests. From an open doorway a Hindu merchant urges the passer-by to enter and look at his wares. There are huge brass trays, silver chains, soft, richly colored prayer rugs and thin little bracelets of elephant's hair, to bring you luck. The air is fragrant with perfume which a shopper is sampling. Outside in the street there is always a chance to buy a marmoset that looks like a monkey, or a bright blue and green parrot. At the street corners or in shady doorways little old women with faces like dried apples hold yards of lottery tickets which they sell to the people passing by.

Panama City looks much like many other Spanish cities. The wide carved doors of the cathedral open onto a central plaza filled with tropical flowers, tall palms, and broad-leaved almond trees. Stone buildings mellowed with age stand on the other side of the square. Narrow streets lead out to the sea wall, down to the open market, and over into Ancon on the Canal Zone. But once a year, for three days before the beginning of the Lenten season, Panama City puts aside work and joins in its carnival. For three days and nights the streets are gay with music and dancing and bright costumes. Spanish lords and ladies mingle with clowns in ruffles, ragged beggars, and bold pirates.

Then the city relives the gay, carefree colonial days.

Seven miles beyond Panama City, near the ocean, stands an ivy-covered wall. Close by is an arched bridge. They are reminders of the old city of Panama which the ruthless Morgan and his band sacked and burned almost two hundred and seventy years ago. But one of the most prized treasures of old Panama was saved from the greedy band. Early in the morning the cathedral bells clanged their warning of Morgan's approach. Quick-witted priests hastily covered the golden altar in the cathedral with white paint and the invaders passed it by. It was not until 1904 that the city felt safe in removing the paint from the gold. Today you may still see the golden altar in the little church of San José, which stands at the edge of a small quiet park in Panama City.

Few of the thousands of travelers who yearly pass through Colon and Panama City know the country that lies beyond the Canal Zone. Panama is about the size of West Virginia. Its deposits of gold, silver, copper, and iron are still undeveloped. Few roads connect its forests of rich cabinet woods with the ports. Small

Photo by Ewing Galloway, N. Y.

PANAMA CANAL. PEDRO MIGUEL LOCKS WITH GAILLARD CUT IN THE
DISTANCE

handicraft factories are its only industries. Bananas,
cacao, coconuts, and mother-of-pearl are its chief exports. Tourists are one of its main sources of wealth.
Labor on the canal provides its most important em-
ployment.

Although it is but thirty-seven years since the

United States undertook this tremendous engineering job, the idea of a canal across the Isthmus goes back through the centuries. Lured by the tales of gold, the handsome and fearless Balboa first crossed the Isthmus to find the chieftain who possessed the gold ("Baskets full, bags full") and who ate and drank from golden vessels. The distance was not far in miles but it was hard going. With a little party of men he forded streams, struggled through swamps, and cut his way through dark forests to scale the mountain from which he first saw the calm waters of the Pacific. A few days later with drawn sword and uplifted banner he waded into its waters and claimed it in the name of Spain. It was Balboa who first thought of the ship canal as early as 1517. At first the King of Spain favored the idea and even ordered a survey of the land, but later he dropped the matter.

Meanwhile the Isthmus had become the pathway over which great riches were carried. The thin-faced Francisco Pizarro who had been with the little party of men who had crossed the Isthmus with Balboa had conquered and robbed the Incas in what is now Peru.

Ships laden with their gold and jewels anchored at the Pacific while donkey trains carried the rich booty across the Isthmus to the ships waiting to bear it to Spain. They were a rich prize for pirates who sailed the Caribbean or lay in wait for the galleons as they turned homeward. A century and a half passed. Many nations discussed a canal and even drew up plans for it. Bolivar, South America's great liberator, dreamed of a free canal built as a co-operative effort of the Americas. On its shores the capital of all the Americas would be built. But his dream was never realized.

When gold was discovered in California in 1849, Panama again became a pathway for searchers eager for wealth. In May of the following year construction of a railroad across the Isthmus was begun. It was completed five years later and shortened the trip by boat and rail from New York to California by more than three weeks.

Meantime France had built the Suez Canal uniting the Mediterranean and the Indian Ocean. Flushed with success she turned her eyes toward Panama, and dreamed of a canal uniting the waters of the Atlantic and Pacific. The Suez Canal is a hundred miles long. A canal across Panama would be half the distance. It sounded simple. Moreover, Ferdinand de Lesseps, builder of the Suez Canal, would do the job. So France secured from Colombia the right to build the canal. (The present republic of Panama was then a part of Colombia.)

De Lesseps arrived in Panama with his family and was given a rousing welcome. People rushed to entertain him and the banquets and receptions were on a grand scale. When work first began on the canal, his young daughter turned the first shovel full of dirt.

But the French had overlooked the fact that the job, though half as long as the Suez in miles, was many times more difficult. The route of the Suez lay across level sand. The Panama Canal would have to be cut through mountains and across tropical jungles. Nor were these the only barriers to be overcome. The worst battle would be fought—and lost—against disease. Malaria, yellow fever, typhus, and dysentery lurked in what was then called the worst plague-ridden spot of the world.

PANAMA CANAL. DAM AND SPILLWAY AT MIRAFLORES

It took courage for new recruits to join forces with the French to replace those who had fallen. Every man who arrived on the Isthmus knew that his chances of escaping yellow fever were slender; that one out of every three who took it would die. More Frenchmen died at work on the canal than were lost during the Napoleonic wars. Daily, long funeral trains crept across the Isthmus. Whenever possible, ship captains skirted its fever-infested harbors.

But while the engineers and workmen struggled heroically against disease, the purchasing agents in France recklessly spent the funds for the canal. There are many tales of the ridiculous things that reached Panama during construction days, only to lie untouched in some warehouse. It is said that one of the purchases included 15,000 torches to be used in a parade when the canal was opened!

For six years the French struggled against the mounting obstacles before they abandoned the idea of building the canal. De Lesseps, who had been hailed as a hero, faced the world a failure and lived a lonely outcast until his death five years later. But although the world branded the project a failure, the American engineers who finally built the canal had great respect for the work of the French engineers.

Although a United States commission made a careful survey for a possible canal, there was little interest in this country for building a canal in Panama. Most people favored a Nicaraguan canal. A little later, however, something happened to change their minds. When the Spanish-American War broke out, one of our battleships, the *Oregon,* was in the Pacific, but it was badly needed with our forces at Cuba. Although it headed homeward immediately, two months passed before it completed the long journey down the west coast of South America, rounded Cape Horn, and headed northward to join the battle. Americans who had followed the slow progress of the *Oregon's* journey were convinced that a canal across Panama would be a good thing. Soon after, the United States paid the French company forty million dollars for its investment and got the Panama Railroad thrown in. For another ten million plus an annual rental of two hundred and fifty thousand dollars we secured from Panama full control—but not ownership—of the Canal Zone.

Two great scientific discoveries made in the meantime were to help bring the canal to completion. Dr. Ross had found the cause of malaria and Walter Reed had proved Dr. Finlay's theory that yellow fever was carried by the mosquito. But although they knew what caused the diseases they were still left with the gigantic task of controlling and preventing them. Colonel Gorgas, who had helped rid Havana of yellow fever, came to the Canal Zone to take charge of sanitation. Mud and filth were breeding places for germ-bearing mosquitoes, and fever raged. Nineteen persons died of yellow fever in June and workmen rushed to the ports to sail for home. But there were no boats, and fearfully they returned to their work, and some to their death.

Slowly swamps were drained and filled in. Brush was cleared and ditches dug. Something of the task may be imagined from the cost, which was sometimes as much as ten thousand dollars to clear a single acre. But the work went on. In September, four months after the June panic, the last death from yellow fever occurred on the Canal Zone. From one of the worst pestholes it was changed into a place famous throughout the world for its cleanliness and low death rate. Proud though Colonel Gorgas must have been of what had been accomplished, he understood the hardships which the French had to endure and was generous in his sympathy. "I think," he said, "it is due the French

Photo by Ewing Galloway, N. Y.

PANAMA CANAL. EMERGENCY DAM AT PEDRO MIGUEL LOCKS

to say that we could not have done a bit better than they if we had known no more of these tropical diseases than they did."

Meanwhile engineers tackled "the biggest job ever completed by man." Colonel George Goethals, the third chief engineer appointed for the canal, saw it through to completion. But tremendous obstacles

93

blocked the pathway of the canal. Miles of tropical jungle, bottomless swamps, and volcanic mountains stretched between Colon on the Atlantic side and Panama City on the Pacific.

But the work continued. The waters of the Chagres River were dammed to form a huge lake, eighty-five feet above sea level, providing twenty-four of the fifty miles of waterway to cross the Isthmus. But ships do not climb hills without help. At Gatun, seven miles from the Atlantic entrance to the canal, locks were built to raise vessels to the lake level. Ships were towed into the first lock chambers, then raised to the level of the second lock by admitting water through little culverts in the lock walls. This was repeated in each lock chamber until the ship finally steamed out on Gatun Lake, eighty-five feet above the level at the Atlantic entrance.

A native village stood in the pathway of the waters which would pour out to form the lake. Again and again the engineers ordered the natives to move, warning them that soon the waters would sweep through the village and cover their homes. But they shook their heads and gave always the same answer. "The waters of the Chagres never rise so high." Once the waters began to flow into the village they fled. A few remaining doubters were rescued from the treetops.

Beyond Gatun on the way to the Pacific engineers set to work to excavate the nine-mile Culebra Cut (later changed to Gaillard Cut) through the ridge of the Continental Divide. Once through, the ships would have covered approximately forty miles of their journey to the Pacific. But before steaming out onto the blue waters of the Pacific, they would have to be dropped the eighty-five feet they had been hoisted at Gatun Locks. Thirty feet of this drop would be made at Pedro Miguel's one lock, just beyond Culebra. At Miraflores Locks, two miles farther, they would be dropped another fifty-five feet to tidewater, then steam on the remaining seven miles to the Pacific.

Meanwhile armies of laborers set to work to build towns on the Canal Zone to quarter the employees. Bordering on Colon and built on land made out of the sea is New Cristobal. A fringe of graceful coconut palms follows its sea wall that leads past the statue of

Christopher Columbus and an Indian Maiden. Balboa and Ancon border Panama City on the Pacific side. Between the Atlantic and Pacific a number of smaller villages edge the canal.

The prado in Balboa is outlined with long rows of stately royal palms. In villages as well as larger towns there are club rooms, swimming pools, playgrounds, restaurants, commissary, dispensary, post-office, and station.

Everywhere there are flowers and beautiful trees: the palm, broad-leafed breadfruit, and lovely frangipani. The Ancon Hospital is famous throughout the world in its treatment of tropical diseases.

But what singles the towns of the Canal Zone out from any in the world is their cleanliness. Every nook and corner is spick and span. From a pesthole it has become one of the most healthful spots in the world.

Year after year the attention of the world was centered on this little stretch of land near the equator. Would the canal be a success, or would it fail? But at last after years of careful planning and painstaking work it was ready. In the White House in Washing-

MODERN STREET IN PANAMA CITY

ton, President Wilson pressed the key and the waters were turned into the canal. The following summer on August 15, 1914, it was opened to the commerce of the world. Its total cost was $396,863,593. Placed on a train of flat cars, the material excavated from the canal would encircle the earth four times.

Completion of the canal had drawn the Americas

nearer in time to the United States. On the waterway journey from New York to San Francisco it cut 7,873 miles, 3,747 miles from New York to Valparaiso, Chile, and more than 6,000 miles from New York to Callao, Peru. On a trip from Liverpool to San Francisco, the canal reduced the journey by 5,666 miles.

Ships and cargo of practically every nation in the world have benefited by the canal. More than 100,000 commercial ships have passed through it since its completion, and the tolls have amounted to more than the building cost.

Once again after a quarter of a century, the Isthmus relives something of the old construction days as suntanned men hack their way through the jungle to build another set of locks. The new locks will provide a waterway for the enormous new ships built since completion of the canal. And should anything happen to halt traffic in the present canal, the new set of locks will be used as a substitute. Today the military forts that dot the Canal Zone, the naval and air bases, are all being strengthened to keep unharmed this key to the security of the hemisphere.

6

IN SOUTH AMERICA—PERU, CHILE, ARGENTINA, BRAZIL, URUGUAY

IT was examination day in Franklin School and the teacher wrote the first question on the blackboard. "Where is South America?" The youngsters read it and smiled. "A snap question," they all thought. Bending over the clean white sheet of paper before them they quickly wrote, "South of North America," and almost added, "of course," so sure were they of their answer.

But is it? Draw a line through from Detroit, Michigan, and extend it straight south. What happens? It just clears Cape Pariña, Peru, the westernmost point in South America, proving that all of South America lies east of Detroit. But, you may wonder, does it matter much if South America is east or southeast of

North America? It is important to us now because the eastern coast of South America is much nearer to Africa, for instance, than it is to the United States. In Africa, England, France, and Italy have colonies. Before the World War of 1914-1918, some of these belonged to Germany. All of these European countries are thickly settled. They need food for their people and raw materials for their mills and factories. South America, which the airplane has drawn so close to Africa and Europe, is a very large continent. Locked within its mountains are unmeasured stores of wealth —gold, silver, diamonds. Besides there are great deposits of minerals important in peacetime and absolutely necessary in war. These countries would be a rich prize to a nation looking for a place in which to expand.

Ten American nations make up the continent of South America, plus three little countries tucked in at the top of the map which aren't American at all. They are the three Guianas and belong to Great Britain, the Netherlands, and France.

There isn't space in one book to describe each country, so we have chosen five of the most important: Peru, Chile, Argentina, Brazil, and Uruguay. Peru, like Ecuador, Bolivia, and Paraguay, has more Indians than white people and many of the same customs. Argentina, like Uruguay and Chile, is almost all white; and Brazil, the only one of the Americas which speaks Portuguese, is a mixture of many races. In meeting them even briefly you will see how different they are from each other, how incorrect it is to think of them as one big country.

PERU

The story of Peru stretches back through many centuries, farther back than that of any of the other nine countries of South America. Its riches have written many of the chapters. Three centuries before Columbus set out on his first journey, the Incas had built their great empire there. Compared even with our own modern day, they were a remarkable people. Most of them were farmers and even then cultivated their fields as modern farmers do today. High up on the mountainsides their fields climbed in terraces like those in some of our Western states. They built great reservoirs and stored water to irrigate the crops when the long dry spells parched the fields.

One of their greatest skills was road building. Excellent highways connected all the important points in their far-flung empire. It included not only the Peru of today but Bolivia, Ecuador, northern Chile, and part of Argentina. Over these hard-surfaced highways relays of fleet-footed royal messengers rushed messages from one end of the empire to the other. Sometimes their route took them for miles across hot, parched deserts. Sometimes they scaled the high Andes by way of staircases cut into the precipice walls. Often they ran in darkness through the long tunnels bored through solid rock. Crossing deep chasms and roaring torrents they sped over bridges woven of maguey fiber that swung like a hammock at every footfall. Surely the runners who could deliver a message to Quito, Ecuador, fifteen hundred miles from Cuzco, and return with an answer in twenty days would have made stiff competition in a track meet!

The sun-loving Incas built their capital at Cuzco,

high in the Andes. Remnants of the wonderful stone temples still stand today. But the sheets of gold and silver which covered the walls have long since been stripped away, and the golden chairs on which the dead rulers rested were snatched from under them by the Spanish conquerors. It was the tales of these riches that lured the thin-faced, hawk-nosed Pizarro southward to conquer the Incas and claim Peru for Spain.

Once again Peru is building roads. For centuries the Andes Mountains, which run like a solid wall the length of the country, divided it into three parts and kept each a stranger to the other. Only donkey paths, sometimes on mountains more than three miles high, connected Lima, the capital, with the mountains and the forests beyond. A trip to Europe was shorter in time and more comfortable than a journey to the interior of their own country. But the skill of Peruvian engineers outwitted the mighty Andes. Today Lima is beginning to eat bananas brought from her own plantations near the jungle rather than from Ecuador. But it wasn't a simple job these engineers faced. Within ninety miles the road that leaves the warm

PLAZA IN LIMA, PERU

port, Callao, at sea level rears up to 16,127 feet and year-round snowfields. Here, five hours from Peru's capital, is the home of the Indians who make up almost three-fourths of Peru's population. Here the women still cut their clothes after patterns their ancestors used. Plump or skinny they all look the same size in the many petticoats that bulge out from their

Courtesy of Grace Line

STREET IN CUZCO, PERU

little tight jackets. Their red felt hats crisscrossed with tinsel look like enormous plump pies tilted on their heads. Chubby-faced babies in bonnets peep out of the shawls on their mothers' backs.

The Peruvian Indian does not worry over the cut of the suits this season. He, too, borrows his ideas from his ancestors. His trousers reach only to his knees and his short jacket has an embroidered scroll around it. His hat is a heavy felt, high in the crown and looking a little as though it belonged to someone else. He wears a thick, warm *poncho* and leather sandals protect his bare feet from the stony mountain paths.

In the high Andean villages the Indians live in a little world of their own. Most of them still speak the Indian language. Few of them know Spanish. Their wants are simple. Many of them are desperately poor. Their meals are a round of the same food with never a change. They dig the mines, build the roads, work the plantations, and make up the rank and file of the army.

Once a week they bring their vegetables and fruit, weaving and pottery, leather and woodwork to the town markets. Nowhere in Peru is there a finer market than the one at Huancayo. In the half-light of early dawn on Sunday morning, the Indians patter through the cobbled streets that lead to the great central market. The women carry bags and baskets and babies. The men struggle under the heavy weight of bags of grain, loads of heavy pottery and leather. Some

PERUVIAN WOMAN AND BABY

arrange their vegetables and grains and fruits in little mounds on the ground and squat before them. Others display their wares in booths or stalls. There is the shoemaker with his piles of shoes and sandals with the designs carefully worked into the leather. Even on market day he goes busily on making more. Beyond him a booth spills over with the weaving that the Peruvian Indian does so well. There are warm heavy *ponchos,* the color of coffee with thin stripes running through them. There are white blankets bright with colored figures. There are brown and white rugs made of llama and alpaca wool and there are yards and yards of orange, green, lilac, and red homespun cloth. Farther on, women sell bundles of wool and little shawls.

Bright red and orange and blue boxes and trunks of all sizes are crowded together near the long row of rush-bottomed chairs. The old woman selling spoons and little llamas made of silver chats with another busily embroidering leaves and flowers and creeping vines on the sleeves of a blouse. The tinsmith hangs his lanterns at the side of the booth and props frames for pictures and mirrors near them. There are mounds of gourds, which make lovely little bowls, with quaint little figures marching over them—men playing games, gay parrots, sulphur-colored tigers with bold black stripes, monkeys swinging from trees, and llamas with their heads held high, their tiny pointed ears taut as though trying hard to listen. Everywhere there is color, the babble of tongues, snatches of songs, and the harsh music of a victrola with a scratchy needle.

This is the market that the Indian loves. It is his holiday at the end of a week of hard work. Offer to buy his heavy load of pottery or weaving or grain at his home and he refuses, for then what excuse would there be to go on to market?

Many years ago Humboldt the great naturalist visited Peru. He crossed the Andes and pushed into the hot, thick jungle in the upper Amazon valley where a fourth of Peru lies. Only about five per cent of Peru's people live there, most of them half wild tribes of Indians, said to be head-hunters. Fever and poisonous insects and slimy serpents lurked in the jungle. But even then Humboldt called it the world's storehouse because it had rich resources and fertile soil. Today, trucks roll over the Andes and down to the jungle, and planes dip in and out. Fever can be conquered and serums fight poisons. The forests are rich in cabinet and dyewoods; the fertile soil can grow rubber and sugar and tropical fruits. Already oil wells are being sunk. But the engineers who put the products of this "storehouse" within reach of the world still have high hurdles ahead of them.

The Peruvians of the rugged highlands and jungle beyond are as far removed from the Peru of the coast as our own hillbillies are from Fifth Avenue. This little strip of coast, fifty miles wide, forms a long narrow edge from north to south. It is not a big part of the country as size goes. Less than a fourth of the people live there. But they are the Spanish Peruvians, the proud families descended from the men who followed Pizarro. They still live in the old family mansions where portraits of their grim-faced ancestors crowd the walls. Beautifully wrought iron grilles bar their windows and heavily carved doors opening onto the side-

Photo by Ewing Galloway, N. Y.

AIR VIEW OF CALLAO, THE MOST IMPORTANT SEAPORT IN PERU

walks shut off a view of patios bright with flowers. Sometimes you catch glimpses of the families as they linger on the balconies overhanging the street or ride quickly through the streets on their way to church or the movies. Beyond the center of the city, wide avenues lead to Lima's suburbs with their modern houses and sunlit gardens.

More than four hundred years have passed since Pizarro founded Lima, "The City of Kings," and named it so because the day was January 6—Three Kings Day. For over two hundred years it was the capital of all the Spanish empire in South America. The wealthy families suited their lives to the name of the city and lived like kings and queens. Ships from Europe brought beautiful furnishings for their houses and the elaborate costumes they wore to their round of parties. When they traveled they went to Europe. Many of the children were educated in European schools.

Lima stands on the flat desert bordering the sea. We think of deserts as hot and parched. But the coast of Peru is not hot. The Humboldt Current beginning in the icy Antarctic flows northward there, cooling the coast and often shutting it off in a thick fog. But now and then, though not often, the hot current coming from Panama reaches down as far as Peru and then it rains. The desert turns green and the poor little mud houses dotting the desert crumble under the downpour. Rivers tumble down the mountainsides and cross

INDIAN AND LLAMA IN THE HIGHLANDS OF PERU

the desert but only ten reach the sea. The others dwin-
dle to nothing in the parched desert. Irrigation ditches
lead water from the rivers to the cotton fields, the
sugar plantations, and the rice fields. But cotton is
Peru's biggest crop and its greatest export. Each year
more acres of blossoming cotton cover the coastlands,
and each year the whirr of more spindles is heard as
the textile mills increase in number. Once again Peru

is clearing matted grass and tangled brambles from the sites of gold and silver mines abandoned when the price of the metals was low. But in the story of modern Peru there will be fewer pages, perhaps, on gold and silver and more on cotton, sugar, wool, and vanadium, needed in making steel. And the modern story may devote many chapters to the Indian, who may play an even more important part in the country's future.

CHILE

Chile would be a puzzling place to a traveler suddenly set down in the country without knowing where he had landed. If his first view of the country was the barren, brown north he might guess he was in the midst of the Sahara Desert; a fog-bound, rain-swept icy morning in the extreme south, with its forest and fjords and islands, might make him think he was in Norway. But California would surely be the guess of the visitor who first saw the fertile fields and the blossoming orchards of central Chile. And if he continued on southward for another 600 miles he would come to the lake region of Chile, "South America's Switzerland."

Many of the Chileans are blond and blue-eyed and look more like people of northern Europe than Spaniards or Portuguese or French. Certainly the names of many of the government officials and the owners of the large *haciendas*—Edwards, Mackenna, Lyons, and Ross, to mention a few—sound Irish or Scotch rather than Spanish. They are names that were brought to the country years ago by a few English, Scotch, and Irish settlers who chose Chile as their new home. Indeed, Chile's first president and national hero was Bernardo O'Higgins, whose father was born in Dublin.

Every Chilean school child can tell you, as well, of the first O'Higgins, famous in South America's colonial days. Born in Dublin, he gave up his studies for the priesthood and set sail for South America with packs of goods to sell. He landed in Argentina and found a good market. But O'Higgins loved adventure and before he had sold everything he decided to cross the Andes into Chile. Everyone told him it was impossible to make such a trip. That decided him to do it. He loaded his packs on a mule, rode another, and after a long, hard trip over the rugged, bitterly cold Andes, he reached Chile. With his faithful mules he traveled up and down the country, poking into parts never seen by most native Chileans. The rest of the story sounds like a best seller written by Alger. For years later this pack peddler became Viceroy of Peru, then the highest post in Spain's new world. Later, when Chile became an independent nation, it was O'Higgins's son who was honored by being chosen the first president.

There are Basque names, too, among the wealthy ruling class in Chile, for it was from the Basque country in the Pyrenees Mountains that many settlers came to the country in colonial days.

Chile's people, like those of its neighbors—Argentina and Uruguay—are mostly white. Few if any Negro slaves were brought to the country in colonial days. Although the Spanish soldiers married the Araucanian Indian women, and many present-day Chileans have Indian blood, still as a nation it is more white than

116

Photo by Ewing Galloway, N. Y.

SANTIAGO, CHILE

Indian. The pure Indians have kept to themselves as a separate nation. Year after year they fought the Spanish colonists until Spain finally made a treaty with them by which they were left a free people to live in the southern part of the valley, still their home today. They have fertile fields of vegetables and grains and some of them have flocks of sheep and ride good horses. From the wool of sheep they weave long-napped rugs and ponchos, and from the silver found in Chile they fashion jewelry. More and more they are laying aside their picturesque costumes to don modern dress. Still you see these costumes along the road as the people go to market. The women wear many skirts, woolen shawls held together in front with flat silver buckles, silver earrings dangling from their ears and a silver necklace about their throats. The men in baggy trousers walk with them, high boots fitted with spurs, rough coat, and a warm poncho of yellow, brown, black, or gray, or perhaps a combination of those colors, and a low-crowned narrow brimmed hat tops off their costume.

Today the Araucanian Indians are gradually becoming a part of Chile's national life. Their lands passed from parents to children, generation after generation. But now and then when there was no one to inherit it, it lay idle. By agreement reached with the tribes, the government is taking over any idle land for white settlers. But the Araucanians are intelligent and are ever watchful of their rights under the new agreement.

In the last few years chiefs and hundreds of their people have ridden northward for conferences with the white Chileans. And once there they have not hesitated to speak out to defend their lands and their customs.

A "shoestring" nation some people have called Chile, because it is so long and so narrow. Beginning at Peru's southern border, Chile runs for more than 2,500 miles between the Pacific Ocean and the Andes Mountains. In some places it spreads to a width of 225 miles. In others it dwindles to but a few miles across. Someone has said that Chile looks like the leg of a North American Indian's trouser, with the fjords at the southern tip forming the fringe. Sometimes you hear that Chile's head is burning with fever while its feet are icy cold. This is because the northern part is but seventeen degrees below the equator and the farthest southern tip is washed by the icy waters of the Strait of Magellan. If the country were laid on top of North America, the top would rest in the middle of Canada and the lower end would touch somewhere near Mexico's southern border.

We have seen how different parts of Chile are from each other. The barren, northern desert, where the rain rarely falls and where neither tree nor flower nor blade of grass grows without irrigation, holds rich mineral stores. Near the surface in this vast barren land lie the rich nitrate deposits which have brought so much wealth to Chile. It is the only country which possesses this mineral needed as a fertilizer and in making munitions. Lack of rainfall turned northern Chile into a parched, leafless desert, but it prevented the nitrate from being washed out of the soil and preserved it to make fertile the fields in other countries. Farther south beyond the nitrate fields, where the Andes Mountains rise highest are the rich copper mines which put Chile at the top of the list of countries exporting copper. There are also mines of iron, lead, and manganese and of gold and silver.

In this northern section there are few rivers even on the western slopes of the mountains. And where there are no rivers there is no water for irrigation and not even a garden surrounds most of the nitrate and mining settlements. All the food is imported, most of it

SKI RUN IN THE LAKE DISTRICT OF CHILE

by way of Antofagasta, the seaport. Only in an occasional valley are there farms and perhaps a tiny village. Many of these canyon farms are shaped like the country itself—long and narrow. They are off the railroad and only donkey paths connect them with the outside world. Most of these farms are owned by the people who live on them and help work them. The workers in the mines and nitrate fields come and go according to the amount of work to be done. Whenever the mines close down, or when there are few orders for nitrates, thousands of workmen return to their homes farther south or even to other countries. Many of the mines are owned by United States companies and a large number of the office workers and officials come from North America.

Nearly a third of Chile lies in the far south, a place little known in the rest of the country. Dense fogs hang over it most of the time, rains drench it almost daily, and icy blasts whip its shores. Thick forests cover parts of it. No roads connect it with central Chile 1,200 miles away. For centuries this far southern region was almost unknown. Only the daring pirates from

Europe fought their way around the stormy Cape.

On the eastern slopes of the Andes, still in Chilean territory, the climate is milder and in the south are the great sheep ranches, many of them stretching over thousands of acres. Few families live here and most of the laborers are brought in from outside and live in huge barrack-like buildings. But the Chilean government is trying to settle this country and knows that the best way to accomplish this is to replace the transient laborers with families. They hope in time to divide these enormous ranches into many small farms, owned and worked by families. It is one of the few chances which the landless Chilean worker has of owning his own home.

Of the entire country, central Chile is the most important part. It is not a large area compared with the rest of the country. In length it is not more than 500 miles. Its width is scarcely more than 200, often not that. But more than three-fourths of the people live here; nineteen of Chile's largest cities are located here, including Santiago, the capital, and Valparaiso, the most important harbor.

123

There is little here to remind one of the barren north and the forest-clad, fog-bound south. Fertile fields stretch between rivers that tumble from the snow-covered Andes. And when spring comes to the valley the orchards are fragrant with blossoming peach, pear, apple, plum, and many other fruit trees. Great vineyards cover acre after acre.

The great estates in Chile are owned by a few hundred families. The owner's house of twenty to thirty rooms is set in the midst of grounds as well-kept as a park. Most of the estates have swimming pools and tennis courts and plenty of fine riding horses, for Chileans are good horsemen. And the snowfields of the lofty Andes are each year more popular for skiers. Teams from the United States have traveled south in the last few years to try their skill on the dizzy slopes. Despite the notion that South America is all a tropical land, there is skiing in many places all year round. Beyond the lawns and flower gardens are the vegetable gardens, the orchards and vineyards.

But often the owner of the *hacienda* is a professional man or a government official with his office and another

Photo by Ewing Galloway, N. Y.

MINING FOR COPPER IN CHILE

residence in the city, where he and his family spend most of their time. An overseer is left in charge of the *hacienda* to supervise the work of large settlements of laborers—often from forty to fifty families—that live on the large estates. Most of the workers were born on the estate and their parents and even great-grandparents lived there before them, perhaps in the same house. As children their lives perhaps followed a set pattern. When springtime came to the central valley the boys may have driven the sheep and cattle to the mountain to graze during the summer months. Perhaps a few older shepherds went with them. The days were lonely high in the mountains, for the shepherd's family stayed below on the *hacienda*. Now and then someone brought provisions from there. And while the boys herded the flocks, the little girls were learning the many tasks to be done around the great house. From their mother or grandmother they learned to spin and weave and sew. They learned how to prepare the food and to preserve that left from the harvest; how to serve the table and to keep the house and to care for the children of the master's family. Later when the boys were older they had other tasks. Shortly after dawn they were in the great fields, where they stayed until sunset when the mountains showed purple in the distance.

Sometimes they made holidays of their work. Once a year when the cattle and horses were brought in to be branded there was a big rodeo, with many days of dancing and games and daring riding. The Chileans love horse racing and always on holidays and Sundays they gather to match their horses' speed. Threshing is another annual event to which the laborers and their families look forward. Today on the large, modern estates there are threshing machines, but still all join in the work. On the smaller estates they still follow the old custom of bringing half-wild horses from the mountain pastures and driving them back and forth over the sheaves of grain until the ripe kernels are trampled out. Afterward there may be races or games and feasting.

But though he is free to work where he wishes, the Chilean laborer born on the *hacienda* usually stays there. His wages are so small that he rarely ever has any money. The managers or owners of near-by *haciendas* would not risk offending their neighbor by hiring a laborer if he left the place where he and his parents had worked before him. If he is ill, he is usually cared for at the expense of the master. When he is too old to work, he may stay on until he dies. But he can never hope to own the little patch on which he grows food for his family nor the house in which he lives.

Although he is very poor, the lot of the laborer not attached to a *hacienda,* the "free" laborer, is much worse. Many of them work in the mines, the nitrate fields, or in factories. When times are hard and there is little work, they may have no home, few clothes, and often little or no food.

Like other South American countries below the equator, Chile has summer during our winter. Now that there are more and faster ships between the Americas, products from Chile's fertile valley are shipped for winter market in this country. Two years ago Chile exported more than 12,000 tons of apples, 1,600 tons of melons, and more than a thousand tons of fresh

COPPER SHEETS IN THE YARDS OF THE CHILE COPPER COMPANY

grapes. Wine is another export that ranges from two and a half to more than three million gallons each year. Grains—wheat, barley and oats—are other big crops from central Chile. Meat, hides, and wool are exported from the grazing region of the far south.

Industries are increasing in Chile, for the country has both water power and coal but still lacks money to develop them rapidly, although already Chile is producing much of the goods needed in the country.

Santiago, the capital, has a population of more than 800,000. It stands in a valley facing the low coast range of mountains and in sight of the Andes that rise behind it. Two hills within the city have been made into lovely parks. One, San Cristobal, is topped with a large statue of the Virgin. The other, Santa Lucia, is covered with wide spreading pepper trees and bright with tropical foliage. It was at the foot of this hill that Pedro de Valdivia and his soldiers founded the city on February 12, 1541. Santiago has fine old buildings dating back to colonial days, and many modern ones that look like those of any of our own busy cities.

There is a story that the Inca Indians called Chile "cream of the land." Today its fertile valleys, the beauty of its lakes and mountains, make it a fitting name.

ARGENTINA

"The most progressive country in South America" is the title Argentina claims for herself. To prove it

Photo by Ewing Galloway, N. Y.

BUENOS AIRES, ARGENTINA

any Argentinian will swamp you with facts. It has the most miles of railway, the greatest number of factories, exports the most products. It is South America's greatest agricultural country and the most industrialized one as well. Its capital, Buenos Aires, is the largest city in South America, and in the entire Western Hemisphere only New York and Chicago are larger. But that is only a beginning. Argentina even leads the world in many ways: she exports more corn and beef than any other country and furnishes two-thirds of the world's linseed. Argentinians claim that *La Prensa* of Buenos Aires is the world's most up-to-date newspaper plant. In wheat and wool Argentina drops to second place, but a *close* second to Canada and Australia.

Visitors to Argentina are usually introduced by way of Buenos Aires, the "Chicago of South America." It is not only the greatest city in South America but a great city in any country. There is little difference between its theaters, its modernistic business houses, fashionable clubs, and busy shops and those of New York, London, or Paris. Its skyscrapers are like the skyscrapers of all the other cities and the electric signs that blaze above them are as bright. It has the same wide avenues filled with the same hurrying crowds. There are the same carefully kept parks. The women's clothes are like those in the latest fashion books and the men's are what the best-dressed men wear everywhere. And like the crowds of most great cities there are people from many different countries—from France, Spain, England, the United States, Italy, and Germany. Many Italians came to Argentina and most of them soon became a part of the country and the people. About a third of Argentina's people have Italian blood. The residential section of the city has homes that look like the homes of wealthy people in New York, London, or Paris. But the shutters in many of them are drawn for most of the year while the owner lives abroad. Buenos Aires is the Argentina that most people know. But it is only one part of this great country. Beyond the city lie the great grassy pampas, plains that stretch on and on until they meet the horizon, and the roads that cross them run for mile on end without a turn. Argentina is as large as the United States from the Mississippi to the Atlantic Ocean.

133

ARGENTINIAN GAUCHO

North to south it stretches over as many miles as separate Havana, Cuba, from Edmonton, Canada.

Enormous herds of cattle and sheep graze on these
grassy pampas. Here the famous Argentine cowboys,
the *gauchos*, are at home. Like our own cowboys, they

were once a very important part of the nation before fences kept the owners' cattle separate. They were a wild lot and the stories of their life make as good movies as our own Western thrillers. They could throw a lasso as surely as Will James or Buffalo Bill, and their eyes could spot their own brand on the cattle as far. Even Hollywood could add little to their costumes. Their baggy trousers were nipped in at the waist under a wide, silver-studded belt. Over them they wore chaps and stuck a long knife in the back of the belt. Their thin shirts blew in the breeze and they tied only the brightest silk scarfs around their throats. A band under their chin held their wide, stiff-brimmed hats in place. Their jangling spurs were of silver and their riding crop had a silver handle. Out on the lonely pampas they sang as they rode and their songs made up as they rode along were not so different from "Get Along, Little Dogies." There are still *gauchos* in Argentina as there are cowboys in Montana, Wyoming, and Texas. But each year they are fewer— and tamer.

Some of these ranches—*estancias* they are called in

Argentina—are as big as a small nation itself. The houses look like castles lifted up out of Scotland and set down on the plains. The broad-leaved eucalyptus trees that surround them make little islands here and there on the long stretches of flat country. There is a saying that even the roosters crow only once on the pampas because they hear no echoing answer.

The fertile soil of the pampas grows the big three of Argentine agriculture: thousands of acres of tall, sturdy corn; great fields of blossoming flax that covers the ground like a pale blue blanket; and acre on acre of ripening wheat fields that reflect the gold of the noonday sun. From its wheat crop Argentina is called "the world's bread-basket." Argentina has still other crops: barley, oats, rye, and birdseed are next in importance to the big three. And scattered over the country are fourteen million acres of alfalfa. Most of it goes into the stomachs of Argentine livestock.

Argentina is south of the equator, so the warmest part of the country is in the north. The same crops grown in our own south thrive there: great fields of cotton, sugar cane, tobacco, and rice. Large orchards

CORN SHELLER ON THE PAMPAS IN ARGENTINA

and vineyards fragrant with blossoms in the spring and ripe fruit in the fall are a part of many of the plantations. But of all, cotton is the coming crop in Argentina.

Because agriculture and stock grazing are on such a grand scale in Argentina they almost crowd out any mention of minerals. But lying deep within the mountains bordering on Chile are stores of copper, manganese, lead, tin, wolfram, and zinc. Oil wells here and there dot the southern part of the country.

What about industrial Argentina? This takes us back to Buenos Aires again, the industrial center of the country. From the crops Argentina grows you could guess at many of its industries. Of course it would have flour mills and sugar refineries. Its textile mills are increasing in number and turn out thousands of yards of cotton, linen, and woolen cloth. Automobiles, radios, farm machinery, and electrical equipment are other growing industries. A country with so many cattle would, of course, have plenty of hides for leather to manufacture shoes. One of the things that gave Argentina the biggest boost was the invention of refrigerator plants. It gives her another first as the greatest exporter of chilled beef. More than 350,000 people are working in industries which manufacture goods for home use.

There are people who think that Argentina will some day become a great industrial nation like our own country. There are other people who don't agree.

GAUCHOS ON THE PAMPAS

They say that Argentina has very little coal and iron—two things necessary for industries. They agree that it has great water power, but say that it is too far from the industrial area. Lack of money to invest and not enough people to buy the manufactured products are still other arguments they offer. But whether it will or will not become a great industrial nation, one fact remains. In the last twenty-five years it has developed more rapidly in industry than any other country.

Why does Argentina of all of the Latin American countries present such a different picture today? Different people give different reasons. Some say it's because she has no great mountain barriers and others say it's because she has no Indians. Still others say immigration has helped her. But whatever the answer it must take us briefly to Argentina's past.

The Spanish settlers in Argentina did find Indians, but they were not the highly civilized, agricultural Indians of Mexico, Guatemala, and Peru. Like the Indians of North America they were a roving race, depending for a living on their skill at hunting and fishing. The Spaniards saw that they could expect neither work nor wealth from them. And soon most of them went the way of our North American Indians. The few left today live in the cold southern tip of the country.

But Argentina needed laborers to work her fields. They encouraged people from Europe to come to make their homes there. Thousands poured in, most of them from Spain and Italy. They settled on the land and became the middle class of the country. But the immigration idea did not work out as in the United States where the immigrants bought their own little farms and worked them. In Argentina the immigrants came in as tenant farmers or as laborers and had to compete with the natives who received very little wages. For despite the need for farmers and the great stretches of land, there is a land problem in Argentina. Enormous plantations are owned by people who prefer to live in some other place—in Buenos Aires or Europe. They are worked by tenants or sharecroppers who cannot hope to buy land of their own.

Argentina of all the American Republics is most like our own country. And when you read more of its history you will find many more ways in which we are alike.

BRAZIL

If you can picture a country as big as the United States would be if it had two states of Texas, then you have an idea of the size of Brazil, the American neighbor who speaks Portuguese. The United States of Brazil has twenty states, a Federal District, and one territory, and every South American country except Ecuador and Chile touches its borders. It has many altitudes, many climates, and immense stores of rich minerals. Almost any crop will grow in its fertile soil. Its great coffee plantations cover thousands of acres and earn for Brazil the title "coffee pot of the world." For mile after mile the coffee trees stand in long, straight rows, sometimes as many as eight million on a plantation. Their narrow green leaves have a newly varnished look. Never are they more lovely than at blossoming, when they are covered with fragrant white star-shaped flowers. Later, when the coffee is ripe, the deep red berries snuggle against

HARBOR OF RIO DE JANEIRO, BRAZIL

the green leaves like Christmas holly. Day by day whole families of coffee pickers—father, mother, and children—strip the red berries from the trees.

Coffee trees demand much attention. When they are young they need broad-leaved banana trees near by to shade them from the bright sun. Laborers pull the weeds and cultivate the earth around the young trees.

Hundreds of people work with the berries after they are picked.

Some of these coffee plantations are as large as one of our states and are complete little communities. The homes of the owners are huge, large enough for the family and all the aunts, uncles, cousins, and grandparents. Brazilians are hospitable people, and sometimes thirty or forty people sit down to a meal in the great dining room. Instead of one patio, the houses have three or four, and the immense storerooms have food enough for a small army. There are big swimming pools, tennis courts, and beautiful gardens and orchards. In hundreds of small houses grouped here and there on the plantation live the laborers and their families. Railroads and telephones connect the different parts of the plantations and the villages are complete with stores, schools, churches, hospitals, and police station.

Coffee hasn't always been Brazil's greatest export, however. Once it was rubber. In the steaming jungles of the Amazon, rubber trees grew wild. No other place in the world, as far as anyone knew, had rubber trees, and the world depended on Brazil for its supply of rubber. Armies of laborers hacked their way through the hot jungles and tapped the trees. The milk from the trees was caught and boiled down into solid balls to be shipped out of the country. The life of the laborers was hard. Fever and poisonous snakes and insects lay in wait for them in the jungles. They worked long hours and were poorly paid. Factories in the United States and Europe needed rubber for tires and raincoats and rubber shoes and the many other things made from rubber. Only Brazil could supply the rubber. The price went up and up and the owners made many millions of dollars. Sleepy little towns far up the Amazon suddenly snapped to life. Within a few years they doubled and trebled in size. Men built palaces for homes and bought anything that came to their mind. They built a million dollar theater and imported people to entertain them.

Meanwhile Brazil guarded the rubber trees. They were the goose that laid the golden egg. No one was allowed to take seeds of the rubber trees from the country. But one day an Englishman returning to his coun-

try hid away in his baggage, safe from the port in-
spector, 70,000 seeds. They were planted in England
and carefully tended. Then the little seedlings were
sent out to the Malay States where the climate was
very much like the climate of Brazil. Labor was cheap
and the plantation owners hired thousands to tend the
rubber trees. It wasn't long before these trees were
producing much more rubber than the wild trees in
the Brazilian jungles. With other countries raising rubber, the price dropped. Brazil was in for a hard time.
While the price of rubber was so high every laborer
in the country had been put to work to gather it.
The fields lay idle and the wealthy people imported
food that cost three and four times more than if it had
been grown at home. Now there was little food and
very few orders for rubber.

Today Brazil is planting more different kinds of
crops. With her soil and climate she has a wide choice.
Cotton thrives in many parts of the country, and already Brazil is producing all the cotton she needs with
enough left over for export. Textile mills, the most
important industry of the country, have been built,

Photo by Ewing Galloway, N. Y.

WASHING FOR DIAMONDS IN A BRAZILIAN STREAM

and already Brazil is making almost all of her cotton goods.

If Brazil has great wealth in agriculture, she also has fortunes in mineral deposits. Nearly one-fourth of the world's supply of iron lies near the surface and a loan from the United States will help Brazil develop it. In addition there are around five billion tons of coal in the

147

country, though it is not a very good quality. The immense supply of manganese ore is of particular interest now for its use in making steel. Tungsten, mica, nickel, crystal, and bauxite are also part of Brazil's wealth that has scarcely been touched. Perhaps to avoid some of the trouble other Latin American countries have had, Brazil passed a law that prevents anyone but her own people from working the mines.

Nestled in the hills of Minas Gerais, the town of Diamantina dreams of her brilliant past. Once the country around produced more diamonds than any place in the world. Then production shifted to another part of the world. Africa became the diamond country and the little town was left with the memory of her greatness. But once again the world is turning to this region for industrial diamonds—*carbonados*—used in making very fine drills. Brazil has semi-precious stones, too. The most important are emeralds, aquamarines, beryls, garnets, topazes, and amethysts. Early in the eighteenth century Brazil staged a gold rush as thrilling as our own days of forty-nine. Many deposits of gold haven't even been worked and before long Brazil may produce as much gold as South Africa.

Brazil has its name from the dyewood found there. *Pau Brazil,* the Portuguese called it, then shortened it to Brazil. Not the least of its resources is its million square miles of every kind of timber, including rich cabinet woods.

Much of this great nation with its fertile acres and rich mineral store is unknown to us. But there is one spot we recognize because we have seen so many pictures of it. That is the harbor of its capital, Rio de Janeiro. High mountains surround it and Sugar Loaf Mountain, the great rock rising out of the bay, stands guard over its entrance. Sugar Loaf is as much a part of the picture of Rio as the Statue of Liberty is of New York. There was a time, though, when Rio was a fever-infested spot, as bad as Panama in the early days. A clean-up program carried out by Dr. Oswaldo Cruz rid the city of yellow fever and made it one of the cleanest and most beautiful in the world.

"In the South American grand opera, Rio de Janeiro is easily the leading tenor," is the way one Frenchman described the capital of Brazil. No other city in the world has a more beautiful location. Older than any city in the United States, Rio's history is as color-ful as its setting. It is a city of more than a million and a half people. It has wide tree-lined avenues, modern business blocks, and bustling, noisy markets. It is a city of fine churches built in the colonial days and palatial residences built in its boom days. It is a city of flower-filled squares and of blossoming gardens. It is a great modern city where people stroll instead of rush, and where they pause in their work to drink many cups of its famous coffee. Hugh Gibson, in the very fine book he wrote about Rio, tells this story about coffee drinking as it is practiced there. A man who was not noted for his energy told an American woman that he drank as many as forty cups of coffee each day. The woman was horrified and said, "But doesn't it keep you awake?" "It does help," the man answered.

"Brazilians like us" you often hear people say in the United States. Perhaps it is because we drink so much of their coffee. Or it may be because they are cordial people and like almost everyone. Perhaps that is why in the streets of Rio you meet such a mixture

Photo by Ewing Galloway, N. Y.

AIR VIEW OF SÃO PAULO, BRAZIL

of races and all of them are treated as equals. You remember that unlike the other American nations (except Haiti) Brazil wasn't settled by Spaniards. A Portuguese explorer named Pedro Cabral discovered Brazil in April, 1500, and claimed it for Portugal. When, later, the Portuguese settled there, they did not find wealthy Aztecs and Incas like those in Mexico and

151

Peru. Indian laborers were used on the great plantations and their lot was much like that on the Spanish plantations. Later, Negro slaves were brought in from Africa to replace the Indians. Ever since, a large part of the population has been Negro and a mixture of white, Negro, and Indian. But in Brazil the different races and classes got along more peacefully than in the Spanish colonies. Brazil has never drawn the color line as we have in our own country.

Brazil had few people for such a vast country and what it needed most was farmers to cultivate the land. The government encouraged people from other countries to settle there. Thousands swarmed in from Italy, Portugal, Spain, Germany, and Japan. The Italians, Portuguese, and Spaniards fitted easily into the Brazilian way of life. But the Germans formed a little Germany in southern Brazil. They had their own schools where until two years ago only German was taught. In the towns most of the shops have German names. They read newspapers printed in German, and they see movies made in Germany. The streets are full of people speaking German, and the schools are filled with fair-haired children, only now learning Portuguese.

São Paulo, most productive of the Brazilian states, is also its industrial center. It has many textile and hosiery mills, and it has flour mills, glass factories, iron foundries, and steel mills. The manufacture of cement is another growing industry and will probably furnish all of the country's needs within a few years. Meat-packing plants are taking care of the country's large supply of meat already on the export list.

URUGUAY

Sometimes we remember countries because they are so much like others we already know. But we will probably remember Uruguay because it is so different from most of the other Latin American countries. First of all it is the smallest of the ten South American countries. But it has proved that small nations like small people may still accomplish important things. Today it stands out among the South American countries not because of its size but because it is one of the most progressive countries. And many of the things it has accomplished give it world importance.

In its appearance as well as in its achievements, Uruguay has a personality all its own. Unlike many of its neighbors, Uruguay has neither mountains nor deserts nor jungles. Someone has spoken of Uruguay as a garden planted between Argentina and Brazil. It might be a very large garden, for there is scarcely any part of the country, except a little sandy stretch of coastland, which cannot be turned into field or forest or pasture. Great fields of wheat and corn and flax cover hundreds of acres of rolling country. Vineyards march up the sides of sunny, rolling hills and orchards of lemon and orange trees produce fruit for distant markets. Vegetables grow well in the temperate climate of the south, but where the country borders on Brazil in the north, tropical fruits and plants thrive.

For centuries Uruguay's vast grasslands have been the home of enormous herds of fine cattle and sheep. Here, too, the *gaucho,* the daring rider and the fearless fighter rode the range by day and at night sang around the glowing campfire. And it was one of these *gauchos* who led his people in their fight for independence.

PRINCIPAL STREET IN MONTEVIDEO, URUGUAY

Like the cowboys of Argentina and our own country, fences and other modern inventions have cut short much of their work. But still their descendants are on the ranches. Now and then you may even see a small group in the costume of the colonial days—bright shirt, gay scarf, silver-studded belt. Now and then they sing the old songs and dance the native dances.

Today Uruguay counts her cattle in the millions— nine million is the latest estimate—and her sheep total more than 20 million head. Its frozen meat industry is one of the world's most important and its meat-extracting plant has earned for Uruguay the title of "the biggest kitchen in the world." Millions of pounds of wool from its sheep place it among the great wool-exporting countries of the continent.

Montevideo is Uruguay's capital, its largest city and its most important seaport. It is a city of 680,000 people, outgrown from colonial days. Founded in 1726, it follows the old Spanish pattern—narrow streets, cheerful plazas surrounded by churches, and public buildings and homes built around colorful patios. But Montevideo's modern section has little of colonial days about it. Its business houses and public buildings might fit into the most up-to-date block of New York or Chicago or San Francisco. Its lovely parks, well-planned suburbs, and excellent bathing beaches give it a place among leading Latin American cities.

In Uruguay there are none of the Indians who are so much a part of many of the other Latin American countries. Neither are there any Negroes. Most of the people are descendants of Spanish settlers and of immigrants—from Italy, Spain, and Germany. All of them quickly adapted themselves to the country and its traditions, and today the people of Uruguay are among the most patriotic in the world.

There are several reasons why this little country has developed into a progressive nation. For one thing, it learned early to take care of itself. Its next door neighbors were huge countries. Argentina was more than fifteen times its size and Brazil is forty-six times as large. For years first one, then the other, tried to take it over. But the fiercely independent *gauchos* of Uruguay were good fighters, and never for long did the larger countries keep their smaller neighbor under control. Finally, in 1828, they gave up trying and recognized Uruguay as an independent state.

But many years of hardship lay in store for the little republic. The people, who had fought so hard to keep their country free, turned then to fighting each other. It was a long, bitter struggle that began with a dispute between two of the leaders for independence. The people took sides until the whole country was divided. For many years the civil war continued and when it was finally over no one was quite clear just what they had fought about. But meanwhile, the country had made little progress. People had fled into Argentina or other countries and the population had dropped by many thousands.

Then, in 1904, Uruguay elected for president a man who has been called "the most remarkable statesman of the whole American continent." His name was José Batlle y Ordonez. With the same daring that his forefathers had shown in defending the country, President Batlle set about to make it a better place in which to live. How well he and the men who followed him have succeeded is shown in what they accomplished.

Today Uruguay's workers have an eight-hour day. They have accident insurance for workers in industries. Child labor is not allowed. Old people receive pensions. Elections are decided by secret ballot and women are allowed to vote. Capital punishment has been abolished. Uruguay has more than 1,500 free primary schools, good secondary schools, and universities. In addition the government supports a School of the Air, to reach those among the rural population who can neither read nor write. These are some of the many important things which Uruguay has accomplished in a little more than thirty-five years.

7

BY LAND, SEA, AND AIR

ON August 10, 1940, the S.S. *America* sailed slowly down the Hudson River. Her red, white, and blue stacks gleamed in the noon sunlight and her whistle blew a hoarse answer to the salutes of other ships in New York harbor. Newest, largest, and most beautiful of American ships, it was bound for a visit to Cuba, Haiti, and other Caribbean ports. By radio, reports of the colorful sailing flashed to the American neighbors.

Only a week earlier a huge "stratoclipper" lifted itself from the blue waters at Miami and flew into the morning sunlight. That same night its passengers slept in Port of Spain, Trinidad—1,900 miles beyond Miami. Blazing a new skyway over the Brazilian jungle the clipper landed its passengers at Rio de

Janeiro after twenty-eight hours of daylight flying time.

Meanwhile in 1939 almost 12,000 motorists sped across the Rio Grande on the Pan American Highway.

On land, sea, and in the air the Americas are drawing closer together in travel time. Silver-winged clippers fly high above the rugged trails of Cortes and Pizarro. In the Caribbean Spanish galleon and pirate vessels have given way to luxury liners. Streamlined automobiles have replaced the lean brown Indian runner.

The air route between Key West and Havana was the first link in the great chain of airways which now connects the Americas. A few years ago Colonel Lindbergh left a cheering crowd at Miami to blaze a new air trail between the United States and Panama by way of Yucatan and Central America. A few months passed and other planes followed the same trail to Panama, then winged their way southward. Planes have brought Santiago, the capital of Chile, sixteen days closer to the United States in travel time. Larger and faster planes were built. More miles were added to flight schedules. Planes span the distance between

New York and Lima, Peru, in two days. Another day's flying time brings you to Santiago. The same flying time connects New York and Rio de Janeiro. Only three and a half days by plane separate New York and Buenos Aires.

Some strange cargoes have flown through the skies between the Americas: baby chicks, tropical flowers, and strange animals for northern zoos. Millions of angry, buzzing wasps from Peru are sometimes flown to Louisiana to destroy cane borers. Their lifetime is short and they would die before the trip could be made by boat. Planes carry medicines between the laboratory and sickroom where the difference in speed may mean life or death. All the chicle taken from the Petén jungle in Guatemala is flown to the Atlantic port for shipment to New York.

The airplane is bringing the United States closer to the other Americas, and it is also helping those countries to know each other. Long, hard journeys separated many of them. Travelers often rode part of the way on a train, then changed to bus or boat, and finished the trip on muleback. But neither rugged moun-

LLAMAS AND PLANE NEAR LIMA, PERU

tain ranges nor bottomless swamps barred the pathway
of the planes. Nowhere have they been of greater service than in Latin America. Commercial flying has developed more rapidly there than in any other part of
the world. Colombia established the first commercial

airway in 1920. Today planes make regular flights over a network of 88,146 miles of domestic and international routes, and connect every country of Latin America. Far in the interior the airplane is no novelty to the Indian who has never seen train or automobile. He may never have worn shoes, seen a movie, or eaten an ice cream soda, but planes are a familiar sight to him. Only a few years ago Indians toiled for weeks over the winding, tortuous mountain trails to carry machinery to the mines where neither rail nor cart roads led. Today huge planes have lifted the burdens from their shoulders and in a few hours fly loads of more than a ton to a trip.

For nine months the Spanish conquerors struggled onward from the west coast until they reached the high plateau of Bolivia. Today a plane covers the same route in a few hours. Traveling by a sure-footed mule across Peru takes three weeks—when all goes well. But a plane will cross it in three or four hours.

Airplanes have cut the travel time between the Americas, but new highways are also helping them to know each other. When the great Pan Ameri-

AN OLD SPANISH SUSPENSION BRIDGE IN PERU

can Highway is finished it will be possible to get in a car at the Arctic Circle in Alaska, drive through Canada and the United States, continue on through Mexico and Central America and across Panama, follow down the west coast of South America to Peru, cross the Andes and end up at Buenos Aires, 16,000 miles and many weeks in time from your starting point. Columbus Day, 1942—the 450th anniversary of his discovery of America—is the date planned for the formal opening. Many people believe that is putting the date too soon. Long stretches of the highway are already completed and have been used for many years now. But some of the hardest work is still ahead in finishing the work on the gaps. They are the hardest problems for the engineers. Some of these stretches are in the jungles, others run through country where tropical rains wash away the grades as they are built. Still other gaps lie in the cold, rugged highlands where the air is thin and laborers working with pick and shovel make slow progress.

One of the outstanding jobs of highway construction is the road connecting our southern border with Mexico City. Crossing deserts, winding around high mountains, dipping into warm, green valleys, and climbing out on broad plateaus, the highway covers a 760-mile stretch. Mexican engineers planned the road and brought in machinery for its construction. But the Mexican laborers said, "Take off the machinery. Give us more jobs." So the machinery was removed

SCENE ON SANTOS-SÃO PAULO RAILROAD, BRAZIL

and the native labor put to work. Most of the workmen were Indians who dislike to work by clock and
whistle. The supervisors wisely assigned to each laborer a certain amount of work to be accomplished—
when it best suited him—each twenty-four hours.
Some rose before dawn and by sunrise had completed
their day's work. Some worked under the burning

noonday sun. Others waited until the blue twilight lay over the valleys. Still others chose to work by moonlight. Day and night little groups swung a pick and shovel until the highway was finally completed in 1932.

Far up in the Guatemalan highlands, in the little village of San Pedro, the Pan American Highway runs into the market square. Red handwoven belts and blue and white shawls hanging outside a little shop all but cover the sign marking the road. On the ground below, an Indian woman sitting before a basket heaped with freshly scrubbed potatoes, bunches of crisp, green watercress, and ripe red tomatoes chats with her neighbor whose wares are neat mounds of peanuts and rows of horses carved of wood. Near by an old man is selling pottery and a wrinkle-faced old woman nods behind her tray of molasses candy. They speak the strange-sounding dialect of the *Quiche* Indians.

Beyond Guatemala City the highway leads southward and finally connects with Salvador, smallest of the Central American Republics. Highways connect Argentina with Chile and Uruguay. Brazil and

Uruguay are also connected by highway. The Bolivar Highway connects the capitals of Venezuela, Colombia, and Ecuador. On the west coast, Peru, the land where the Incas built their famous highways, has made swift progress in roadbuilding. Already the road so long needed to connect Peru north and south is completed. But beyond the Andes engineers push ahead on a road that will some day cross South America. The Cordillera Azul, the last mountain barrier before the road drops to the level land, gave them a hard problem to solve. Some of the engineers thought a tunnel was the only way of crossing the towering range. But the tunnel would need to be a mile and a quarter long, dug more than a mile high. They must find a lower pass, the engineers said. How they found it is a tale that sounds a little like a treasure hunt. One of the engineers searched through musty volumes in libraries which told of early expeditions in that part of the country. Franciscan missionaries had explored the country almost two centuries ago and had carefully set down detailed accounts of their journeys. In one of these books he found the story of their trip

Photo by Ewing Galloway, N. Y.

BRIDGE ON CENTRAL RAILROAD OF PERU. THIS IS THE HIGHEST BRIDGE
THE WORLD

through a gap in Cordillera Azul—exactly what the
engineer was searching for. He noted carefully the
direction, the time it had taken them to make the
trip, and something of what the country around looked
like. Then he and his men started out. For several
months they searched, pushing into country where

Photo by Ewing Galloway, N. Y.

TUNNEL THROUGH THE UPPER PEAKS OF THE ANDES IN PERU

there was no sign that anyone had been before. Bright birds flashed overhead, monkeys scolded them from the treetops, and once a jaguar glided down the mountain only a few yards from where they stood scarcely daring to breathe. At last they found the canyon and began to push on through it. Lashing themselves together with ropes they struggled through the gorge,

171

where someday automobiles will follow them. Beyond they found half-civilized Indians, who were amazed to see these white-faced callers. Bolivar was the name of their chief and he gave them help in exchange for food and clothing and tools.

The pass has been named "Father Abad's Gap" for the missionary who found it years ago. It lies almost a fourth of a mile above sea level and is about two miles long. Walls almost a mile high hem it in on both sides. The determination that drove the engineers on to find the pass saved the country many thousands of dollars and shortened the job of building the highway by many years.

Modern highways contrast sharply with the Camino Real (Royal Highway) which connected Upper California with Mexico City at the end of the eighteenth century. Its construction was due to the dauntless courage and determination of Father Junipero Serra. Almost two centuries ago he stepped from the boat at Vera Cruz, Mexico. Then he began his long, wearisome journey by foot to Mexico City. Plodding onward under the burning tropical sun, wading streams, struggling through dense vegetation, straining up the rocky mountainside, he finally reached Mexico City footsore and weary.

But the hardships of the trip did not discourage him. Soon he began a still longer journey, this time on horseback, to reach Upper California. His second trip was even worse than his first. He suffered tortures from an ulcer in his leg, from fever and fatigue. But he refused to listen to those who begged him to stop, and kept on until he reached his goal. The chain of Franciscan missions he established in California still stand as a monument to his courage and determination.

At the close of the eighteenth century a relay of couriers covered the distance between Upper California and Mexico City. On the first of every month a courier turned southward on the Royal Highway. At each settlement he stopped to gather letters and messages. Then crossing hot deserts, scaling mountains, and pushing on through lush, green valleys, he finally reached the end of his journey. The postman who carried the local mail between missions made a quaint picture. Wearing only a breechclout and carrying a stick with a split in the end where he stuck the letters, he jogged steadily on and covered sixty to seventy miles from dawn to dusk. Today planes rush mail over the same route in a few hours.

Streamlined trains also span the distance between our own country and Mexico's capital. Daily they leave our cities, speed beyond the southern border, cross a stretch of lonely, silent desert. Still rushing onward, the train climbs into the lovely Mexican highlands, zooms past Indian villages, pauses in larger towns, and continues its journey until it draws into the station at the capital, sixty-four hours from New York and fifty-two hours from Chicago. At the southern border Mexican trains connect with the Guatemalan line which runs through banana lands, past plantations of shiny, green-leaved coffee trees, winds through wooded slopes around Lake Amatitlán, and on into Guatemala City. Here still another line leads beyond the border into busy little Salvador.

Although railroads link few of the southern republics, many of them contain lines which are famous in engineering history for the odds overcome in building

174

SCENIC HIGHWAY IN VENEZUELA

them. It took daring imagination and stubborn courage to build the Peruvian Central Railway. To reach its highest point, almost three miles above sea level, it climbs steadily upward between parched slopes, crosses sixty-seven bridges, bores through sixty-five dark tunnels, and uses eleven switchbacks. Everywhere engineers marvel at the skill it took to construct the tunnels, the most remarkable in the world.

Costa Rica has a famous railway connecting the Atlantic port with San José, the capital. The story of its construction is a tale of courage and loyalty. The survey led through fever-haunted country and by the time the first twenty-five miles were finished, 4,000 men had lost their lives. It took nineteen years to build little more than one hundred miles. Money ran low and there was none to pay laborers. But they had faith in the builder, and both Negro and white laborers stayed on the job for nine months without pay. From sea level at the coast the train climbs slowly upward winding through the lovely Costa Rican mountain country. The grades are steep, and when it rains the rails are slippery. Always when you ask when the

176

BUILDING THE PAN AMERICAN HIGHWAY IN MEXICO

train will arrive, the conductor gives you two answers
—one if the sun shines, the other if it rains, which
slows the journey.

Among Brazil's more than seven thousand miles of
railway is a stretch of forty miles called the "Coffee
Railway," which connects Santos with São Paulo.
Only a short distance it travels over flat country,

before heading almost straight up in the air. In six miles it climbs 2,000 feet. But before beginning this climb, the train is divided into short sections of a few cars each. One by one they are hauled up by cable; then they are hooked together again, and the train puffs on into the city of São Paulo. Almost all the coffee exported is hauled over this little line.

Argentina completed her first railway more than ninety years ago and today its 24,000 miles of rail gives it first place in Latin America and eighth in the world. Despite the odds against which they struggled, the southern republics have increased rail mileage from 18,300 to 83,000 miles in fifty years. But they have not realized their dream of a great international railway to connect all of the nations.

For many years sea travel lagged between the Americas. The trips were long and uncomfortable. The traveler setting out from New York bound for Peru had a two-month trip ahead of him. Boats sailed down the east coast of South America, rounded Cape Horn, and turned northward up the west coast. When the Panama Canal was opened it cut more than a month

DIFFICULT CONSTRUCTION WORK ON THE PAN AMERICAN HIGHWAY IN
MEXICO

from the trip. Four years later, in 1918, boats steamed
out of North American ports to begin the first regular
service to the west coast of South America by way of
the canal. But still the sailings were few and slow and

179

passengers made the trip for business rather than pleasure.

Between New York and Buenos Aires and Rio de Janeiro journeys were equally slow and the schedule no more certain. Then in 1938 the American Republics Line launched its "Good Neighbor Fleet" between New York and South America's east coast. The crowded sailings proved how much the line was needed and within a few years larger and faster ships will make the run. On the Pacific coast, four new ships connect this country with the west coast of South America. Nor is the shipping program limited to the United States. Chile has several modern merchant ships and is expanding her fleet and shipyards. On a foundation of forty German boats held there during the World War of 1914-1918, Brazil has built a good-sized merchant marine. Ships flying the flags of other of the American Republics are helping them become better acquainted.

Not long ago a little girl in New York, lonely for her home in Chile, picked up the telephone and talked with her mother near the southern tip of South America. Cables, radio, and telephone bring the Americas within speaking distance of each other and help to make them better acquainted. It is almost twenty years since government officials in Washington and Havana greeted each other over the newly-opened telephone service. Ten years later, President Hoover in the White House at Washington and the presidents of Argentina, Chile, and Uruguay in their own capitals exchanged greetings over a five-thousand-mile radiotelephone circuit. Now telephones connect the United States and all of Central and South America. The telephone has also acted as peacemaker several times within recent years when the opportunity to talk things over has helped to prevent serious trouble between nations.

Thus the modern mercuries of America have made us closer neighbors and are helping us become better friends.

8

WE DEPEND ON THEM

WE are a strong and a rich country, yet we depend on even our smallest neighbors for many things.

Our dependence on the Americas begins with breakfast. Without coffee or cocoa, it would be a dreary meal, indeed. Sugar for our cereal probably came from Cuba and the bananas from any of a dozen of the American Republics. The aluminum coffee pot may contain bauxite from Brazil.

Coffee heads the list in importance of the products which we import from Latin America. Brazil grows more coffee than any other country. From its huge crop it gets the name "coffee pot of the world." Colombia has immense plantations too and is a close second to Brazil in coffee production. Almost all of the coffee

Colombia exports is drunk in the United States. Guatemala prides herself on the quality of her coffee. At the Panama Exposition in 1915, it took the highest award. A dozen other Latin American countries produce coffee. In the years between 1936 and 1938 the United States' yearly bill for coffee from Latin America was $135,220,000.

Most of the coffee-growing countries also produce cacao. An ambitious person estimated that in this country we drink 2,730,000,000 cups of cocoa each year. Almost half of the cacao used in making it comes from the twenty Americas. In addition cacao is used in millions of candy bars, ice cream sundaes, and chocolate éclairs. All of these sweets require sugar. Cuba, "the world's sugar bowl," supplies about two-thirds of all we import. If it should become necessary, the sugar we now import from the Philippines could be supplied nearer home, in Latin America.

Our fifty-million-dollar chewing gum industry depends upon chicle. Most of it comes from the jungles of Mexico and Guatemala. Toiling long hours in the damp hot forests, men drain the milky sap from the

COFFEE PLANTATION IN SÃO PAULO, BRAZIL

sapote tree, cook it until it thickens, and pour it into molds to harden. Once the tree has been tapped for chicle it must have a rest period of seven years before it can be tapped again. The forests where chicle is gathered are far from the cities. Few roads lead into them. Airplanes fly into the chicle country to take the slabs of chicle to the port.

Photo by Ewing Galloway, N. Y.

PICKING COFFEE IN BRAZIL

Imagine a fruit market without bananas. Yet there are people living here today who remember when bananas were first brought to the United States as an experiment. They were a hit overnight and people asked for more. More acres were planted and a fleet of boats fitted out to carry the delicate fruit. Bananas are fussy travelers. They must have just the right temperature to keep them from ripening. For bananas are always

185

Photo by Ewing Galloway, N. Y.

PILES OF COFFEE ON THE DRYING GROUNDS

picked green and are not allowed to ripen until they
end their journey. Ripe bananas would bruise with
handling and would not be fit for market. Now, weekly
liners ride at anchor in a dozen southern ports while
a moving chain of men carries bananas between the
freight car and ship. All of the bananas eaten in the
United States come from the other Americas and our

186

SACKING AND WEIGHING COFFEE IN BRAZIL

annual bill in the last few years has averaged $29,-971,000.

The Brazil nuts which make such a big lump in Christmas stockings come from Brazil, and so does our entire supply of babassu nuts, from which oil is made.

We are likely to forget that the Americas produce

an enormous amount of wool. More than sixteen per cent of all the wool used in the world comes from Latin America. Millions of sheep live on the far-flung plains of South America. Again Argentina claims a world record, for her sheep are said to be the finest. Great quantities of wool are also exported from Brazil, Chile, Peru, and Uruguay.

Early in the morning when the sun first peeps over the Guatemalan mountain tops, long lines of sheep move up the mountainside to graze. Behind them tag little shepherd boys, their warm ponchos pulled close to keep out the sharp mountain cold. Riding through the highlands you come upon little groups of them playing together or sitting in a spot sheltered from the cold wind. The villages in the sheep country are bright with bundles of dyed wool hung to dry. From the open doorways there is a whir of busy looms and on a grassy spot near the house dozens of striped or plaid blankets are spread to dry. They are always washed when taken from the loom.

The alpacas and llamas are another source of wool. "Where the sheep stop, the alpaca begins," is a saying often heard in Peru and Bolivia where most of the alpacas live. They love the highlands and seldom live lower than 6,000 feet. With their wool hanging almost to the ground, the alpacas look as though they wore long skirts. Long ago the Incas in Cuzco offered alpacas for sacrifice, white ones to the Sun and black for the son of the Sun.

Centuries ago many of these countries that produce wool were noted for their weaving. Cloth so finely woven that it was waterproof came from their looms and difficult designs were woven into it without using a pattern. There is a story that some of the Indians, no matter how well they could weave, would always make a mistake in each piece on purpose. They did this because they believed that only the gods were perfect and that they would be angry if the weaver did a perfect piece of work.

Textile mills are increasing in Latin America today and many countries make all of the cloth they need. But they will never make such beautiful pieces as the handwoven textiles found in the tombs of the Incas.

In addition to food and clothing, Latin America

has seven products which are tremendously important to us. We might not have telephones if it were not for antimony. Three countries—Mexico, Peru, and Bolivia—furnish almost all we use. Without tungsten we would not have incandescent lamps. The same three countries furnish this and so do Argentina and Chile. We must have mercury for thermometers and the backs of mirrors. Mexico furnishes it, too. Quartz crystals are needed to make radios and airplane instruments. Coconut shell char is used in making gas masks. Of all these materials, manganese is perhaps the most important. It is necessary in making steel. And automobiles, machinery, modern buildings, battleships, airplanes, and dozens of other things are only part of the list for which steel is needed. Brazil and Cuba are the only two Latin American countries which have large stores of manganese. Cuba also supplies chromium needed in making steel.

Think of the many things for which we need rubber. Automobile tires, for one thing, take a great share of the rubber we use, for we have more automobiles than any other country in the world. Today

BRAZIL NUTS FROM THE AMAZON RIVER REGION

most of our rubber comes from the Far East. But that is far from our shores. Industries that need great quantities of rubber are anxious to get it nearer home. You remember that Brazil was the first country to produce rubber.

Henry Ford bought land in Brazil and planted rubber trees on it. Already some of the trees are producing. The Goodyear Rubber Company has plantations in Panama and Costa Rica.

Agricultural experts think that instead of having enormous rubber tree plantations, it would be a better idea to have small groves of rubber trees on each plantation. All the way from Mexico to beyond the equator the climate is suited to their growth. If the Americas begin producing rubber in great quantity, we will depend even more on them for materials we need daily.

Quinine that we take for colds and fevers is another product of great importance to us. It was first found in Peru. More than three hundred years ago the wife of the Viceroy (Governor) of Peru lay desperately ill. The best doctors in Lima were called in to attend her.

Photo by Ewing Galloway, N. Y.

AVOCADOS FROM BAHIA, BRAZIL

But despite their efforts she grew steadily worse. Then, when all else had failed, someone suggested that perhaps the medicine the Indians made from the bark of the cinchona tree might help. She was given a dose and the doctors waited anxiously to see what would happen. Gradually the fever left her and she was cured. When she returned to her home in Europe she took some of the medicine with her. Ever since, quinine has been an important item in the medicine chest. Without it to control malaria, the Panama Canal might never have been built. The engineers who are working in the jungles today always carry quinine with them. Like rubber, production of quinine has shifted to the Far East, but again Peru is planning in time to supply most of our needs.

Our navy needs millions of feet of rope made from Manila hemp. Today most of it grows in the Philippines. Hemp is a cousin of the banana tree, looks almost exactly like it, and needs the same climate as bananas. But hemp is more easily grown because it doesn't require such fertile soil and can therefore be raised on land worn out by bananas. The United Fruit

Photo by Ewing Galloway, N. Y.

CACAO OR CHOCOLATE PODS GROWN IN VENEZUELA

Company has experimented with growing Manila hemp in Costa Rica and has planted 2,000 acres. Half of it is already producing. The Company hopes to plant 40,000 acres of hemp in Central America.

More than a thousand different kinds of hardwood trees grow in the Americas. Already we get many cabinet woods from them, particularly mahogany. Brazil has over a million square miles of almost every variety of timber. Argentina and Colombia each have more timber than the United States, excluding Alaska.

In addition to products which we need every day the Americas furnish many luxuries. Most of the lovely green emeralds in the jeweler's window came from Colombia. Mines which the Spanish colonists opened four hundred years ago are still being worked. The long wars of independence interrupted work on some of the smaller mines and quickly the jungle covered them. But men eager for the rich green gems are again searching them out from the thick vegetation.

Colombia has platinum, another precious metal, and we take all she exports.

Brazil has rich diamond mines, and valuable pearl beds lie off Panama's coast. Gold that lured the Spanish conquerors and had a great deal to do with the story of the Americas is still found in more than a dozen of the southern republics. No other country in the world produces so much silver as Mexico.

These are some of the well-known products for which we depend on our neighbors. In 1939 we paid

ACAO PODS SPLIT AND SHOWING SEEDS WHICH WILL BECOME CHOCOLATE

the Americas more than 500 million dollars for products we bought beyond the Rio Grande. In turn they bought more than 562 million dollars' worth in this country. What we bought from the Americas amounted to a big bill, but it was only half of what they had to sell.

Since the Latin American countries are agricultural

countries, their exports are agricultural products. Their imports are machinery, automobiles, typewriters, sewing machines, and many more manufactured products. Half of our purchases from the Americas are tropical or semi-tropical products like bananas, coffee, cacao, coconuts, and others which we cannot grow here. The other half of our purchases were products like corn, wheat, and wool, which we bought to add to our own supply. If our purchases of these products became too great, they would compete with our own farmers, cotton planters, and livestock producers, who would object. They say that if we increase our purchases from Latin America, we must buy things which are not grown here.

The other Americas have a great variety of climate and soil and grow many different crops. Experts believe that the problem may be solved if the Americas will develop new crops and increase production of crops they grow now. Already the Americas have experimented in growing products we now buy from other countries. They have proved, for instance, that excellent tea can be grown in Brazil and Guatemala. Other

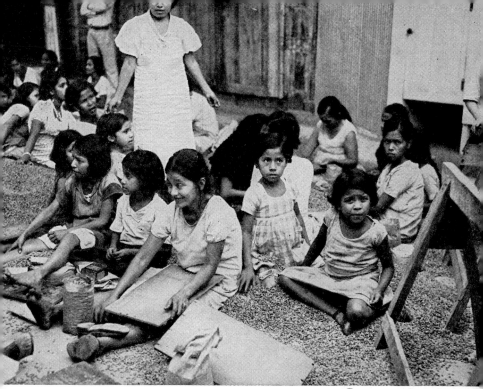

CHILDREN SORTING CACAO IN ECUADOR

products which we need could be grown in the Americas: kapok for upholstering and life-preservers; perfumes and flavoring extracts; ramie, a fiber used for textiles; tagua nuts (vegetable ivory) for buttons, nuts for oils, paints and varnishes, and many other things. Many more products may be discovered through experimenting.

199

Growing more different crops would benefit the Americas. They would not be left with a huge surplus of one or two crops like sugar, bananas, and coffee when foreign countries did not buy. A greater variety of crops would give the laboring classes greater variety in their diet. Tortillas made from corn, red or black beans, occasionally a stew, a little fruit, rarely if ever a vegetable, is the menu meal after meal and day after day for most of them.

9

WE SHARE THEIR CULTURE

ONE morning a small boy with a book in his hand slipped into the front seat in a schoolroom in Guatemala City. The class had already begun. He could hear the children whisper, *"Americano."* It was the only word he understood of the language everyone around him spoke. He could not read the stories in the book which the teacher gave him. Time passed slowly. He had never been so lonely. Then it was time for the art class. He could draw even though he didn't know Spanish. The boy next to him was drawing pictures of Mickey Mouse all over his page. He looked up and smiled and the newcomer felt less lonely. He, in turn, held up the airplanes he had made. When they went out to play his new friend took him by the arm. Things went better.

You could strike a ball a Spanish friend threw even if you didn't know how to talk to him. When they went back in the classroom some of the other boys stopped and looked with interest at his book, although they knew nothing of what it said. Many of the songs the children sang in music class he had heard before. The new teacher played the same march his teacher at home had played. When the day was over half a dozen little boys walked home with him. Although they spoke Spanish and he knew only English, they had become friends by the things they did rather than what they said.

Nations like people can understand each other through the pictures they paint, the books they write, the songs they sing, and the games they play. Already there are people in each of the American nations who know and understand their neighbor nations. There are groups who have worked for a long time for better understanding among the Americas. The Pan American Union which celebrated its fiftieth birthday in 1940 is one of the best known. Each day its experts answer hundreds of questions about the Latin Ameri-

ANCIENT CHURCH ARCHITECTURE IN PERU

can countries. There is never a day when visitors do not roam through its halls to see the bright woven textiles, decorated pottery, cases of brilliant mounted butterflies, grains, minerals, and precious stones brought from the southern republics. People interested in stamps and coins spend a long time studying the collections. And grown-ups as well as children are delighted when the bright blue, green, and red macaw screams at them in his hoarse voice.

Throughout the United States there are small groups interested in learning more about Latin America. But things move swiftly in the world today. If the people want to enjoy the benefits of co-operation with the other countries on this hemisphere there is little time to waste. Good teamwork needs a leader. So the United States government offered to help us to know the Americas and to have them know us. Although this sounded like an interesting task, it would not be an easy one. The people who carried out the program would have to be both wise and patient. For this special work the State Department set up the Division of Cultural Relations. It is not to take the place of the other agencies. It is to help them work together and if possible to avoid repeating the same work.

So, in order to let organizations and people know the plans and to get their suggestions for still others, the Division of Cultural Relations sent out invitations

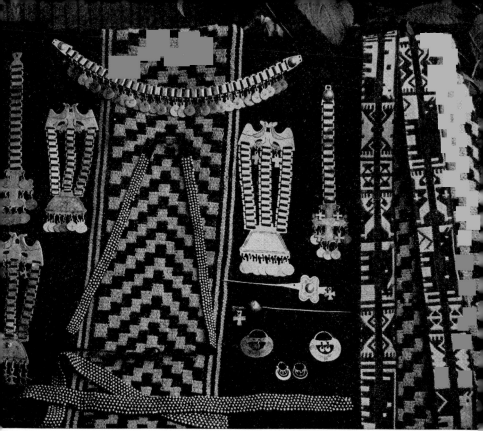

SOUTH AMERICAN INDIAN DESIGNS

to a series of conferences. Artists, musicians, teachers, librarians, writers, and publishers left their work to attend the conferences. Business men who could only be spared from their offices for a short time came too, because they realized the need for knowing the Americas better. From early morning until late night they dis-

205

cussed how best to help the Americas know what each had done in art, music, education, and literature. Already results have proved that the conferences were worth while. One of the important things they did was to answer the question many had asked, "What can these little-known countries give us?"

In 1940 the Virginia Museum of Fine Arts at Richmond had an exhibit of Argentine painting, prints, and sculpture. An exhibit of Mexican arts in New York's Museum of Modern Art helped to make that neighbor better known to us. The large exhibit of Latin American art at the San Francisco Fair delighted the thousands who visited it daily. Plans are under way to send some of our paintings to the other Americas. Not long ago a Brazilian painter, Candido Portinari, sometimes called South America's greatest painter, arrived for his first visit to the United States. The three hundred canvases he brought with him show in vivid colors the everyday life of the working people in Brazil. The Art Institute of Detroit already has some of his paintings. Portinari began painting when he was eight years old when he coaxed a brush

RUINS OF A PRE-INCA CITY IN PERU

from the hands of a painter who was decorating a church and promptly painted steps on the ceiling! Besides being very much interested in our modern art, Mr. Portinari likes our Western movies. One of the things he wants most to see on his trip is a real cowboy.

Costume designers and interior decorators "discovered" the Americas only a few years ago. But the wave of Indian and Spanish designs that has swept over the country since shows that they are making up for lost time. The Mexican's wide sombrero, the Ecuadorean's hat not unlike an inverted vegetable dish, and the Inca woman's headgear that tilts at a dangerous angle have all been copied with few changes. Women dressed in shoes and coats of gay handwoven textiles from Guatemala are no longer stared at as though they were bound for a costume party. In their homes, too, they have pottery dishes and glassware, rugs, furniture, and hangings from the other Americas.

Through music, too, the Americas are becoming better acquainted. Concerts of chamber music played in the Library of Congress have been broadcast by short wave to Latin America. Phonograph companies are making more records of the music of the Americas, especially folk music and dances. Already through the radio we know many of our neighbors' popular and folk-songs. We may not know all the words, but we recognize the tunes of "Estrellita," "La Golondrina," "La Paloma," and many others. Chavez, Mexico's well-known conductor, has been guest conductor of some of our most famous orchestras. Opportunity to enjoy Chavez's music has not been limited in Mexico to those with the price of a symphony ticket. For a dozen years he has given free concerts to school children, workers, and peasants.

Another of Latin America's musicians has been called "the most significant American composer of the twentieth century." Eight years ago Heitor Villa-Lobos began a piece of work which he knows he will never see finished in his lifetime. But that hasn't lessened the great amount of energy he is putting on it. He has undertaken the task of directing musical education in the public schools of Brazil. When he was asked to take charge of this important work, he already

Photo by Ewing Galloway, N. Y.

NATIVE CHILEAN BASKET WORK

had definite ideas on how the job should be done. First of all he wasn't interested in teaching music as a "frill" in education. He believed that taught the right way it was an important subject through which children would learn patriotism, understanding of their vast country, appreciation of its many different people, and respect for people of other countries. That looks like a

MEXICAN BASKET MAKERS

big program. No one realizes that more than Villa-Lobos. That is why he knows that all he can do is to lay a solid foundation and leave others to build on it. One of the first lessons was to teach the children not to *roar* their national anthem, a lesson that we might do well to learn. He taught them folk-songs, a little about musical instruments, and now and then a few dates in the history of music. The courses increased in difficulty in the high schools. Villa-Lobos also plans to have adult schools to teach grown-ups to sing in choruses on national holidays.

In 1940 the All-American Youth Orchestra made its Latin American good-will tour. Chosen by Leopold Stokowski from thousands of young musicians in the United States, they made a seven week tour and visited Brazil, Argentina, and Uruguay, with a short stop at the Dominican Republic. At each of the nineteen concerts which they gave, enthusiastic audiences greeted the young musicians. Everywhere they made friends for the United States and for themselves. Already youth orchestras in Brazil and Argentina are planning a visit to our country.

Still another way of getting acquainted with people and nations is through their books. Several centuries have passed since the first book printed in this hemisphere came out. Still we know few of the books written in the other American Republics, and their bookstores contain few of ours. Two years ago, a committee of book publishers in the United States hit upon an excellent idea. With more than 6,000 books donated by thirty-two different publishers they arranged exhibits and sent them to Rio de Janeiro, Buenos Aires, and Montevideo for about a two weeks' stay at each place. The committee realized that it is hard to know books in glass cases, and wisely gave orders that people were to be allowed to handle the books and look through them. Of all the different sections of the exhibit, the juvenile books were most popular. As a result of the exhibit one of the best-known children's books of South America, written by a Brazilian, has been translated into English and published here under the title "The Story of the Palm Tree." The same year that our books were being shown in South America the American Library Association invited Latin American nations to send some of their books to an exhibit here so that we could learn about their life and customs. The exhibit of 400 books was shown at the meeting of the Library Association in San Francisco, then sent for short stays to a dozen or more cities in this country.

São Paulo in Brazil is building what is to be one of

the finest library buildings in the world. Anxious to have the librarians just as up-to-date as the building, the director of the library came to the United States not long ago and visited many of our libraries. This year two of his staff with the help of the Committee on Library Co-operation received fellowships to study at the Louisiana State University.

While here in the United States we are making an effort to introduce the Americas to this country, they in turn are trying to make us better known in their countries. Few people here know of the fine work of the Cultural Institutes in Buenos Aires and Rio de Janeiro in making our country better known there. They have proved that they know one of the best ways of doing this by giving thousands an opportunity for learning English. Through the help of the Institute of International Education a group of Argentine educators visited the United States about ten years ago and made a tour of schools, libraries, museums, welfare organizations, and industrial plants. Groups from Chile and Brazil also visited the United States.

Last but not least, movies can be helpful in aiding

MEXICAN POTTERY

countries to become better acquainted. Good travel pictures of both North and South America help to correct many strange ideas the nations have of each other. Thousands of children in this country perched on the edge of their seats as they watched the "Adventures of Chico," a movie filmed in Mexico. Chico, the little Mexican boy, won many friends in this country by his quaint speech and quick understanding of birds and animals.

The Cultural Relations Division didn't invite Mickey Mouse and Popeye to its conference, but they have become ambassadors of good will for us in Latin America. A well-known publisher said not long ago: "The comics have conquered South America." Readers there are following the adventures of Charlie Chan and the problems of Bringing Up Father as eagerly as we do. People who laugh over the same things have a good start on becoming friends.

10

AT SCHOOL

IT is early morning. The place is almost any city in Latin America. Well-dressed children, their arms full of books, are hurrying through the streets to school. Eight o'clock is not an unusual hour for classes to begin, and with a two-hour lunch period many aren't dismissed until four in the afternoon. Even then many children hurry on to a class in French or English, or perhaps to take a music lesson. When they have finished high school, perhaps before, many of them will go to school in Europe or the United States. Few of them will have to work their way through school. They are the children of the well-to-do parents. Their fathers own plantations or mines, or perhaps they are lawyers, doctors, or engineers.

Until comparatively recently people in Latin America have had little interest in increasing the budgets for public school education. Even where there were free schools, not all of the children could attend. Often even the very young were needed to hoe the corn and beans, to mold pottery and herd the sheep and goats. Neither had their parents gone to school.

The Spanish colonists had no more than reached the Americas before they looked to their schools. But then, too, it was the children of the governing and wealthy parents who had most of the opportunities for education. The missionaries who came with the colonists established some schools for the Indians. They taught them trades, handicrafts, and religion. There was then as now the problem of the many different Indian dialects and some of the priests learned the Indian language in order to teach them. Often the Indians in the schools were seized to work in the mines or on the plantations. In the difficult days following the wars of independence there was neither time, money, nor interest in carrying education to the ignorant masses.

Slowly, however, the belief that all children of whatever race or class have a right to an education gained ground in the Americas. Modern rural schools are being built to educate the peasant's child, and Latin America is tackling the even more difficult problem of educating the parents. There are many people who speak Spanish but can neither read nor write it. Even the cities have large groups of these. There are thousands of others who know only the Indian tongue of their particular tribe. Many of these live in villages far beyond the towns and cities. Only winding paths traveled by donkeys connect them with the outside world. They have no telephones, no postmen, no radios. But slowly adult education programs are bringing the outside world to these people.

It is evening in a mountain village far from Colombia's capital. Men, women, and children are hurrying through the cobbled streets that lead to the central square. Once there they push as near as possible to the frame which holds a movie screen. As the scenes flash on the screen a man with a microphone explains them. Sometimes there are pictures of the beautiful capital they have never seen, a seaport with modern liners, fields and crops new to them, or another part of the

TEACHERS' TRAINING SCHOOL IN MEXICO CITY

Americas of which they have never dreamed. Sometimes the announcer explains how the crops are grown or the harvest stored. Many other groups like these are meeting in Colombia's little villages. Instead of movies, sometimes there are puppet shows to teach simple lessons.

Village libraries are still another experiment Colombia has tried out in her educational program. These are for people who can read very simple language, about

SAN MARCO UNIVERSITY IN LIMA, PERU

primer stage. The libraries are stocked with easy-to-read books on child education, hygiene, agriculture, literature, history, and many other subjects. Pamphlets on handicrafts, carpentry, cooking were also introduced in the libraries. In order to receive one of these libraries free the village must do three things: the Town Council must be responsible for the library; it

UNIVERSITY OF CARACAS, VENEZUELA

must appoint a librarian and pay him a salary; each year they must include in the village budget a sum, no matter how small, to buy more books. Already Colombia's peasants have benefited from this intelligent educational program.

"The House of the People" the Mexicans call their rural schools. As the name suggests, they are used by

SAN JOSÉ COLLEGE IN SANTOS, BRAZIL

the parents as well as the children. Many of the
schools were built by the people themselves with the
help of the teacher. Here the children learn reading,
writing, and arithmetic. But in addition they are
taught to use tools, tend the school gardens, orchards,
and animals. The mothers come to the school for
classes in child care, sanitation, how to prepare health-

ful food, and to use the school sewing machine. The teachers or sometimes an expert in agriculture helps the father select better seeds, suit his crops to the soil, and to improve his cows, pigs, and goats by better feeding and breeding.

Here in the house of the people parents and children learn the all but forgotten folk-songs of their ancestors. They learn to weave old patterns and to paint old designs; they learn the steps of the dances for the fiestas. This is only a small part of Mexico's rural education program. Men trudge days across rough country to plead for schools for their children, for irrigation ditches, for wells of safe drinking water.

Several years ago in Bolivia two men teachers, who were interested in the Indians and had faith in what they could do, decided to try out an experiment. They began building a school near a village. It was a strange sight to the Indians to see white men doing heavy work like carrying stones for a foundation. They were curious but little interested until they learned that the school was not only for them but that they would have a share in directing it. Then they helped with the work and before long a wing of the building was finished. The two brothers taught reading, writing, and arithmetic, but Indian experts in carpentry, ironwork, and other crafts came in and taught their trades to the children. More children entered the school, some from far away who boarded there. The school was enlarged and more Indian teachers took over new classes. Finally they were given entire control of the school. Indian chiefs travel sometimes as long as three and four weeks on foot to see the work being done here.

These are only a few of the programs for educating both adults and children which the Americas are trying out. The work goes slowly and often in the face of great difficulties, but already the results show what can be accomplished.

But if primary and elementary education have lagged in the Americas, higher education got off to an early start. Long before the Jamestown colonists arrived in our own country, there were many schools of higher learning in the New World. The University of San Marcos in Peru and the University of Mexico were founded in 1551. Harvard, our oldest university, didn't come into existence for another eighty-five years. By 1600 there were eight schools of higher learning in Latin America. Today the Americas have sixty-seven universities.

It is only in recent years that students in Latin American universities have showed an interest in an education that would fit them to hold jobs in factories, mills, machine plants, and in business administration. From colonial days they had crowded into classes to fit them for professions. Medicine and law were first choice. Engineering and architecture came next. Most of them disliked working with their hands and felt that such work required neither brains nor skill. Often the engineers could draw excellent plans but had no idea of doing even the simplest task they called for. Some of the countries had to call on foreigners to supervise their industries.

But already technically trained natives are taking a hand at running the mills and factories and directing construction. Some of them have been trained in schools in the United States. Many more are enrolled in new schools in their own or neighboring countries.

SEEDLINGS OF RUBBER TREES ON HENRY FORD RUBBER PLANTATIONS,
BRAZIL

Another change is taking place in Latin American universities. Many of them are beginning to build campuses like our own and to take an interest in athletics. Their schools have little of the university life as we know it. Glee clubs, literary societies, and school dances were little known. Latin American students were—and still are—intensely interested in politics,

Photo by Ewing Galloway, N. Y.

TAPPING RUBBER TREES IN BRAZIL

and most of their gatherings were to talk over political problems. Even children in the lower grades have heated arguments over their favorite candidates for office in the government.

Many Latin American students have come to the United States to school. They learned our language and our customs and made us better understood in

Photo by Ewing Galloway, N. Y.

CLEARING JUNGLES FOR PRODUCTION OF RUBBER IN BRAZIL

their own country when they returned home. But because the Americas were so little known here, few of our students knew of the fine old schools in the southern republics.

Educators who came to the conference called by the Division of Cultural Relations stressed the value of student exchange in helping the Americas to know each other. At a conference in Buenos Aires in 1936 the American Republics had arranged for such an exchange. By this arrangement fourteen students from the other Americas have been chosen to study in the United States this year. Eight students and three professors from this country have been invited to study in Latin America. Still others are making plans for an exchange.

We were not surprised that students of the Americas sought out our schools. But many here asked, "How could our students benefit by going to school in those countries?" The question proved how little they knew of their record in higher education.

Many of the medical schools in Latin America have done important work of benefit to the world in their treatment of tropical diseases. The Butantan Institute in Brazil is known throughout the world. Ruins of villages, temples, and tombs of the highly cultured races who lived there long before the Spanish conquest make many of these nations rich fields for students interested in archaeology. Furthermore, they will have the advantage of working with men who are outstanding in their profession.

Perhaps one of the most unusual experiments in inter-American relations was tried out by the University of Pennsylvania. Instead of sending students, they transferred part of their regular summer school to the University of Brazil in Rio de Janeiro. Twenty-nine students and two teachers made up the group which stayed for a six weeks' term. Living in Brazilian homes, the students had an excellent opportunity to know the people, and the Brazilians, too, became acquainted with some of their neighbors from North America.

11

AROUND THE CONFERENCE TABLE

O N the calendar of school celebrations, Pan American Day on April 14 has taken its place along with birthdays of heroes and dates of great events in each nation's history. On that day the flags of the twenty-one American Republics are massed together in thousands of classrooms throughout the nations. On that day we commemorate the first meeting in Washington of the twenty-one American Republics in 1890. And that meeting was the beginning of the effort to develop co-operation and understanding between the Americas.

But the idea of Pan Americanism goes back even farther than that. It was first the dream of Simon Bolivar, the liberator of South America. When the long struggle for independence had ended, he turned his efforts toward uniting the newly created nations. He dreamed of a great Spanish-American nation with the capital city on the Isthmus of Panama. And to discuss such a plan he called a conference to meet in Panama in 1826. But it was difficult to travel between the Americas in those days. There were few boats and they were painfully slow. Bolivar spent long, anxious weeks waiting for the delegates to arrive. But of all the twenty-one countries, only four were represented at the conference. The United States had been invited to send delegates, but their departure was so long delayed that the conference was over before the delegate arrived. The other had died on the way.

There were reasons, though, why the Americas showed little interest in Bolivar's idea. The Latin American republics had just gained their independence from Spain. Each had so many problems of her own that there was no time to think beyond her own borders. The United States was busy pushing westward. There was little time to talk about a foreign policy. Besides, communications were poor. Goods were joggled in wagons over rough roads or shipped on flat-

PAN AMERICAN BUILDING, WASHINGTON, D. C.

ENTRANCE HALL OF PAN AMERICAN BUILDING

boats. Trade with the distant markets of Central and South America was still but a dream.

Although few nations took part in Bolivar's conference the idea of meetings between the Americas took hold. Eight different times within the next sixty-two years the Latin American nations met to discuss their problems. The United States, busy with the affairs of a rapidly growing nation, did not attend the meetings.

Then, as our country grew, conditions changed. Our industries developed. Our factories were producing more goods than we could use. We needed new markets to take our surplus, and we looked southward with new interest. A conference of the Americas would be a good thing, we thought. So in 1889 Secretary of State Blaine sent out the invitations. The Dominican Republic alone declined. After long, slow journeys the delegates assembled at Washington in the spring of 1890. There were many fine speeches but little action. The one important achievement was the establishment of a Bureau of American Republics to gather and exchange commercial information. Later the name was changed to the Pan American Union and given added duties.

Two years later a second conference met in Mexico City, and in 1906 the Americas met in Rio de Janeiro. In 1910 Buenos Aires was the meeting place and before the conference adjourned the delegates had agreed to meet again in 1915. But the war broke into the conference schedule and the American Republics did not meet again until 1923. This time they journeyed to Santiago, Chile, for the conference.

Many things had happened since the last meeting of the American Republics. Delegates of some of the nations felt very cool toward the United States. Some of them felt that this country had meddled too much in the affairs of the other American Republics. It was true that we had sent our Marines into several of the countries to keep order. Colombia felt unfriendly because she believed that the United States had helped Panama to gain her independence. Mexico was particularly unfriendly because we had had trouble with her at Vera Cruz and General Pershing had marched into the country to hunt down Pancho Villa. These were a few of the things delegates from the other

American Republics remembered when the conference met in Chile.

The United States argued that we had to keep peace in order to protect the Panama Canal, that it was to the interest of the other nations that we keep order in the neighborhood of the Panama Canal.

Several of the Latin American countries had joined the League of Nations. They were anxious to establish an American League of Nations. That would require unanimous consent and the delegates could not agree. The conference was scarcely under way before it was evident that there would be little agreement on anything. However, one important thing was accomplished. They established a commission whose task was to help settle disputes between the Americas.

Misunderstandings increased in the next few years. The Latin American countries had troubles among themselves over boundaries which had never been clearly marked. And they became more suspicious of the United States. By the time the sixth conference met in Havana in 1928 there was little evidence of the friendliness and co-operation of which Bolivar had

BLASTING IN NITRATE FIELD, CHILE

dreamed a century before. There was even difficulty in agreeing on what the conference should discuss. Once the meetings got under way tempers rose and some of the arguments were so hot that they were not taken down for the conference record. One of the delegates packed up and left before the conference was over. Those who stayed accomplished very little, and practically everyone went home in a bad humor.

Meanwhile Mr. Hoover had been elected President and before his inauguration he visited some of the Latin American countries. When he finally took office he began to withdraw our Marines from Latin America and to follow a policy which President Roosevelt later named the "Good Neighbor Policy." Standing on the Capitol steps on the day of his inaugural, Mr. Roosevelt spoke the words which have since become famous: "I would dedicate this nation to the policy of the good neighbor—the neighbor who resolutely respects himself and, because he does so, respects the rights of others. . . ."

But countries like people have long memories. The neighbors remembered other fine words and promises, some of which were never kept, and they waited to see how the policy would work out before cheering it too much. The first sign that this might really work was seen at the conference in Montevideo in 1933. Secretary of State Cordell Hull headed the United States delegation and his friendliness, sincerity, and courtesy reassured the other delegates. For the first time a conference of the Americas was thrown open to discuss questions of interest to all. Mr. Hull's statement that his country was opposed to interfering in the affairs of other nations was welcome news to the delegates. And shortly after the conference the United States canceled the Platt Amendment which gave it the right to take a hand in Cuba's affairs. A few years later our government and Panama wrote a new treaty in which the United States gave up certain rights we had in Panama.

The next conference was planned for 1938, but before that date President Roosevelt called the American Republics together for a special conference to meet in Buenos Aires. They were as surprised as they were delighted when he decided to attend. Even the children joined in the elaborate preparations to welcome him. Thousands of them learned "The Star-Spangled Banner" and bravely struggled through several verses of it to the accompaniment of a band. President Roosevelt's carefully prepared Spanish greeting was lost in President Justo's wide embrace, as crowds cheered, guns roared a salute, and planes circled overhead. President Roosevelt made but a short stay and left Secretary Hull and the other American delegates to go on with the work. Before the conference ended the Americas had agreed to consult with each other whenever any nation, American or non-American, attempted to interfere with their affairs. The conference also made headway on a program for settling disputes among the Americas.

The delegates met as friends when they assembled in Lima in 1938 for the Eighth Conference of American Republics. They were willing to work together and to do the more difficult thing—to give in when there was disagreement. Already the peace of other countries was being threatened. There were long anxious discussions at the conference. Before the delegates left

Photo by Ewing Galloway, N. Y.

UNLOADING CARS AT NITRATE PLANT

for their homes they had agreed that if ever the peace and security of any of the American nations was threatened, all of the American Republics would unite against the enemy. Furthermore, they agreed that whenever it seemed necessary to do so the Foreign Ministers of the American nations would meet to talk things over and decide what to do. Any one of the American Republics could call such a meeting. Before the year was over war broke out in Europe and the President of Panama asked the Foreign Ministers to meet in Panama City.

Everyone accepted. And when on September 23, 1939, he rose to greet the conference, delegates of all the American Republics were in their places or on the way. Day after day they discussed ways to keep the Americas out of war and war out of the Americas.

One of the first things the delegates did was to declare American neutrality. They created a committee of seven men to study the problem of neutrality and get it into some sort of a workable plan for the Americas. They also created a "safety belt," a three hundred mile wide strip edging the east and west shores of the

Americas. They then gave notice to the warring nations not to enter this zone. From the first people said that couldn't keep ships out. And it didn't. Both German and British ships entered, and all the Americas could do was to write notes of protest. Besides the neutrality committee, the Ministers at Panama arranged for an economic committee with a member from each of the American nations. Its task was to work on problems to do with shipping, trade, and banking problems.

The Panama conference went off very well. Many people thought that the most important thing the Ministers did was to show that they could work together. Then as the year wore on the fighting spread and, at the invitation of the United States, the Foreign Ministers met in Havana to discuss grave problems.

Latin American countries had sold a large share of their coffee, cotton, meat, sugar, and a dozen other crops to England, France, Germany, and Italy. In turn, they bought things from them. Now that these countries were at war they were canceling many of their orders. What could Latin America do with all of these products? And, they asked, if they couldn't sell, how could they buy? Already the people were beginning to feel the pinch of hard times.

Our own country had problems, too. Our factories and foundries and mills, even our hospitals, depended upon foreign countries for materials like rubber, tin, iodine, tea, coffee, and many others. Many of these products could be produced in the Americas. Would they be able to supply our needs? Could we take more of their other crops and increase our trade with them, we asked?

There were other, even bigger worries which the Americas shared. Some of the southern nations, you remember, have big German and Italian populations. If Germany won the war in Europe, would these nations be next on the list? Dozens of little islands belonging to England, France, and the Netherlands dot the waters near the Americas. What would we do if Germany or Italy decided to take them over?

In deciding what to do, nations have just as hard times as people have. But when twenty-one nations have to agree on what to do, it can be almost twenty-

Photo by Ewing Galloway, N. Y.

NITRATES FOR AMERICA AND EUROPE

one times more difficult. The lights burned long into the night as they tried to solve their problems. But the people at home, who followed the day by day reports of the conference by radio and newspaper, saw that this was an unusual meeting. The nations, anxious for their security, were willing to co-operate. Even Argentina and the United States, who often disagreed, forgot their differences and worked together like good neighbors. Before the conference ended the Americas made important decisions which answered some of the questions in their minds when the conference met.

They agreed to set up a committee to deal with anything to do with the colonies. If Germany, for instance, tried to take the islands near the Americas which belong to the countries she had conquered, the Americas would take them over before Germany could get them. Things happen quickly these days. The Americas or the committee might not have time to meet to decide what to do. In that case, they agreed that any one of the twenty-one could go ahead without waiting for the others. You might think that would give countries a chance to go out snatching more territory. They agreed, therefore, that any seizure would be made in the name of all the American Republics, and while they held the colony they would all have a hand in governing it. When the war was over, it would be given back to the country who had owned it, or it would be assisted to become an independent nation.

This was one of the most important decisions made

Photo by Ewing Galloway, N. Y.

NITRATE TANKS IN CHILE

at the conference. It was the one that hit most snags before agreement was reached. Argentina objected at first to such action. The islands in the Caribbean are a long way from her own shores. She disliked the idea of mixing in trouble so far distant, and at first said why not wait and see what happens? A few other countries felt much the same way as Argentina. But the waters of the Caribbean wash the shores of more than a dozen of the Americas. What happens there is of great importance to Panama, Mexico, Venezuela, Colombia, Central America, the island Americas, and, of course, to the United States. They argued that no matter how far removed the danger, the Americas must stick together. The weather was hot and the delegates were tired, but they kept their tempers and finally won over the other nations. Argentina showed, too, that she could be a good loser by agreeing on what was best for the others. People who for years had hoped for better co-operation among the Americas drew a sigh of relief. They felt that the conference was over its worst hurdle.

The conference also agreed that should the German or Italian colonies in the Americas make trouble, all of the American nations would unite to help the countries threatened. Already they have kept their promise. Not long ago the little country of Uruguay heard that the Nazis were planning a revolution there. Immediately Brazil lent Uruguay guns to defend herself. Later, the United States refused to permit a Nazi agent, expelled from Brazil, to stay in this country.

The conference appointed a committee to solve the problem of markets for surplus products and increased trade between the United States and Latin America. At the end of ten days the delegates packed their bags and left for home—still good friends. They had not solved all of their problems, but they had proved that in working together the twenty-one American Republics were "all for one and one for all."

12

IN THE GALLERY OF PATRIOTS

YOU will meet many new faces if you climb the broad marble stairs to the Gallery of Patriots in the Pan American Union Building in Washington. Overhead the flags of the twenty-one American Republics are massed in colorful array and below stand the portrait busts of the men whom the nations have chosen as their national heroes. We need no introduction to George Washington, our nation's choice for this honor. But neither the names nor the features of many of the others are known to us. Like Washington, many of the men whom the American Republics have chosen to take their place in the Gallery of Patriots fought and died to help their countries become independent nations.

Here Bolivar, "South America's liberator," is surrounded by some of the brave men who fought with him. Among these is San Martin, chosen by Argentina as her hero; Sucre, best loved of all of Bolivar's companions and hero of Bolivia; the hard-riding, fiery Artigas of Uruguay; Unanue, the physician and scholar of Peru; Santander, the "Organizer of Victories," whom Colombia honors; and O'Higgins of Chile, the son of an Irish pack peddler who became Viceroy.

It is more than a century and a half since a pale-faced, restless little boy with auburn curls played with his toy soldiers in Venezuela. Moving them here and there, he sent them on long marches or lined them up to meet each other in pitched battle. But the mischievous pranks of the boy who played so earnestly with his soldiers were the despair of the private tutors brought into the Bolivar home to instruct little Simon. One after another they left, some of them after very brief stays, and it was finally his old nurse Hipolito who taught him to write. When Simon was seven years old he went with his widowed mother, a brother, and two sisters to live on one of their vast coffee plantations. For it was a wealthy family into which Simon Bolivar was born.

Finally the family found in Simon Rodriguez a tutor who could handle the boy. The tutor had long opposed the Spanish rule in the colonies. It was Rodriguez who first implanted his ideas of democracy in the boy who was one day to become South America's liberator. When he was a little older he went to Spain to continue his education. For a while he had a fling at the gay society life and some of his many love affairs got him into considerable trouble. At last, disgusted with the useless kind of life his companions led, he turned to his studies. He had been particularly annoyed at the way in which the native-born Spaniards looked down on anyone from the colonies. When his education was finished and before he returned to America, he traveled through Europe. Bolivar returned to Spain before setting sail for his home and succeeded in winning permission to marry the beautiful girl with whom he had been in love while he was a student there. She lived but a short time and when she died Bolivar, only nineteen years old then, stayed on his plantation

Photo by Ewing Galloway, N. Y.

STATUE OF BOLIVAR IN CARACAS, VENEZUELA

mourning her. Later he returned to Europe and it was then that he met Francisco Miranda, a fellow countryman who had long been working for South America's independence. Bolivar returned to America, more than ever determined that his country should gain its independence.

From that day until South America's Spanish colonies won their independence, Bolivar gave every effort to the struggle. And in 1824 when the last victory was won and the red and yellow flag of Spain was hauled down in South America, Bolivar had helped to free the land that was to become the republics of Venezuela, Colombia, Ecuador, Peru and Bolivia, the latter country named in his honor. But his was not a steady march to victory. Now he won brilliant victories and the next moment tasted bitter defeat. Exiled from his country, the man who was born to immense wealth lived in a miserable rooming house in Jamaica and was ragged and half starved. From Jamaica he went on to Haiti and with the help of the President there he organized the expedition which he led to Venezuela.

But Bolivar was not interested alone in helping the countries gain their independence. The dream he kept always before him was the union of these countries into a single great nation. The progress of the nations, he said, depended upon co-operation. Now, a century after Bolivar, the Americas are learning how wise were his words. Bolivar's bitterest disappointment was that so little interest was shown in the conference of American Republics which he called to meet in Panama in 1826. Long anxious months he waited, refusing to believe that the delegates would not arrive. Bolivar did not live to see his dream realized, but he had laid the foundation for Pan Americanism. When Bolivar completed the liberation of Peru, no honor was too great for the people to heap upon him. Everywhere he was greeted as a great hero. People fought for the honor of entertaining him and children strewed flowers in his path as he rode through the streets.

Bolivar had always a deep admiration for George Washington. Among his most prized possessions were a medal and a locket containing a picture of Washington together with a lock of his hair, sent to him by Washington's family.

He was president of Peru; then held the same high office in Colombia. Later, when he made himself dictator, his friends turned against him. Unhappy and discouraged and in poor health, Bolivar resigned his office and died a few months later. Today, not only Venezuela but the whole world honors his name.

Streets, avenues, parks, and public buildings are named for Bolivar.

Little José San Martin was five years old when Bolivar was born. Down in Argentina he, too, played with his soldiers and sometimes carefully held his father's sword. He, too, was a problem for his teachers, because he liked to play hookey from class. When José was only eight, his father, an army officer, returned to Spain. There the boy attended the famous Seminary of the Nobles and began his military education which he was one day to use against the Spanish forces in the colonies. As soon as word came of Argentina's declaration of independence he left Spain to fight for his country.

San Martin began to train the army which he finally led on the march which even today seems impossible. Heading his troops, they began the long, hard climb to scale the steep, rocky, snow-crowned Andes Mountains separating Argentina and Chile. For five weeks they struggled on over a route which today planes span in as many hours. But the Spaniards were

STATUE OF JOSÉ SAN MARTIN IN CARACAS, VENEZUELA

taken so much by surprise that they were defeated in two quick victories and Chile was added to the list of independent nations. Today military men still marvel at the courage and determination of a leader who could accomplish such a march. When the grateful people of Chile offered him the presidency he refused it so that their own native son would be chosen. San Martin immediately began preparations to invade Peru by sea. A few years later this, too, was accomplished and he accepted the position of head of the Lima government. But independence had not yet been won. There were large Spanish forces in the Peruvian highlands. San Martin's small forces were no match for them and he called on Bolivar to unite with him to complete the liberation of Peru.

It was then that the two men who had done most to break the power of Spain in South America met for the first time. No one is sure just what took place at the meeting. They can only guess that Bolivar refused to share the leadership with San Martin, and so, because he put the cause of independence before his own ambitions, San Martin left the leadership to

Bolivar and set sail for Europe. He died in Spain when he was seventy-two, without having again looked on the lands which he had struggled so hard to free. To-day his name is written high on the role of America's heroes.

In the army of courageous, determined men who followed San Martin over the high Andes was Bernardo O'Higgins, a native of Chile, who fought to free his country from Spanish rule.

His father was born in Ireland and had risen from a pack peddler to Viceroy of Peru, the highest position in the Spanish colonial service. Bernardo's mother was Spanish. The first school the boy ever attended was one established by his father to educate the Indian chiefs. When he was nine years old Bernardo entered a school in Lima and seven years later he was sent to London to finish his education.

Often his father's agents forgot to send him funds and he had to earn money by copying manuscripts and translating. Even the man in whose care young Bernardo was placed kept most of the money sent for the boy's expenses. One of the accounts contains a bill of sixty-four dollars for the year's supply of shoes. But actually Bernardo's shoes were so worn that his toes stuck out.

Then, quite by chance, he met the man who was to set him on the path which finally led to his country's independence. A Venezuelan soldier who was earning a poor living by tutoring in London, answered Bernardo's call for someone to help him with his mathematics. The tutor was none other than Francisco Miranda, who was then in London trying to raise money and aid to free Spain's colonies from the mother country. Miranda spent most of the mathematics lessons talking to Bernardo about freedom and democracy. Later, on his way home, the young boy met San Martin in Spain.

When O'Higgins returned home, his father was dead and he lived on the plantation with his mother and sister Rosa to whom he was devoted. The same determination, which drove his father on to scale the towering Andes with his pack mules, later forced the son over the same mountain wall with San Martin to liberate his country. Tired troops, heartened by his wild daring, pushed on to victory. He was given the presidency which San Martin had wished him to have as a native son of Chile. Then he turned to aid San Martin in building the navy and later sailed with him to invade Peru. When San Martin retired to Europe, O'Higgins stayed on to help Bolivar complete the work of independence. He headed the government of Chile until 1823, when a revolt broke out and he was forced to resign and flee the country. He found refuge in Peru, the country he had helped free, and died there twenty years later when he was sixty-five years old. Today Chile honors the fearless leader who fought with San Martin to win her independence.

"If God should give men the right to select the members of their own family, I should choose Sucre for my son." This is how Bolivar expressed his affection for Bolivia's national hero, Antonio José de Sucre. Best beloved of all of Bolivar's commanders in the war for independence, Sucre was born of wealthy parents in Venezuela in 1795, and was but fifteen years old when he enlisted to fight for independence with Miranda and was exiled to Trinidad with his commander. Four years later, when he was nineteen, he came under Bolivar's command. Sucre was a diplomat as well as a military man, and it was he who helped arrange the armistice that ended the war in Colombia. The terms of the treaty have been called the "most beautiful example of mercy applied to war." Later his brilliant victories won independence for Ecuador and for a year he stayed on as the governor of the country. Still, today, the people of Ecuador love and respect his memory.

Sucre's next victory was at the famous battle of Ayacucho, which finally broke the rule of Spain in South America. Later when the Republic of Bolivia was organized, Sucre was chosen as its president for life. But he unselfishly refused the long term and accepted the high position for only two years. Willing to assist wherever he was needed, he next led Colombia's army to aid Ecuador when Peru tried to take part of that country on June 4, 1830, when he was but thirty-five years old. The same year, as he was crossing the mountains on his way to Ecuador, a shot fired from behind a tree struck Sucre and killed him. He was only thirty-five years old when he died, but in that short life he had accomplished more than most men accomplish in a life twice as long.

In a schoolroom in Uruguay there once hung a picture of George Washington which bore the well-known phrase: "First in war, first in peace, first in the hearts of his countrymen." But schoolboy champions of their own national hero wrote in a bold hand after it: "Artigas is the best and the greatest!" From early kindergarten days they had heard of his daring deeds, how the people had loved and followed him. It is one hundred and seventy-six years since José Gervasio Artigas was born in Montevideo on June 19, 1764. His grandfather had been one of the founders of the city and his family was prominent in society. Young José was educated in the schools of the city and then went to work on his father's ranch. He loved the ranch and the life of the *gauchos*. He rode with them and sang with them around their evening campfires. The country people loved and respected him, and later were ready to follow him in the fight for independence.

In 1810 when Argentina began its fight for independence from Spain, Artigas resigned his commission in the Spanish army and took his place with the rebels. With a small band of one hundred and fifty men he set out to free Uruguay from Spanish rule. Immediately hundreds of *gauchos* and country people among whom he had lived joined him, and a few months later they won a victory over Spanish troops. When they took up the fight to drive the Spaniards out of Montevideo, some of the Argentine troops that had been helping them fell back, and Artigas was forced across the Uruguay River into Argentina. But he did not go alone. The rural people who loved him left their homes to follow him. Men drove herds of cattle before them, women carried pots and pans and bundles of clothes and followed in a great caravan behind their beloved leader. More than three-fourths of the people in the entire country settled with him where he made camp. Nowhere in history has any leader been given such proof of his people's affections.

INDEPENDENCE PLAZA IN MONTEVIDEO, URUGUAY

The deeds and ideals of Artigas reached our own shores when he wrote his ideas of democracy to the Argentine Assembly. At that time President Clay said: "The only champion of democracy in that region is the brave and chivalrous Artigas."

Five years after he first rode at the head of his little band of men, Artigas occupied Montevideo and reached the peak of his power. But the brave little country had but a short time to enjoy its victory. The next year the Portuguese pushed into the country, determined to take it for Brazil. For four years Artigas and his followers held out before they were crushed. He found safety in Paraguay and died there thirty years later. But although he did not lead his country to its freedom, his deeds have lived on in the hearts of the people who chose him to take his place in the Gallery of Patriots.

Far up in the highlands of Peru almost two centuries ago, a little boy studied his lessons in catechism and Bible History. Hipolito Unanue first began the studies which were to prepare him for the priesthood in the Seminary in Arequipa. Later he joined his uncle, a priest who taught in the University of San Marcos in Lima. When his uncle saw that his nephew was little interested in a religious life he urged him to study medicine.

Young Unanue was good-looking, intelligent, and had a pleasant personality. He made friends easily and was a favorite among the people who gathered at the home where he was tutor. But Unanue did not spend all of his time in society. Ten years after he first came to Lima he passed the examination and was chosen Professor of Anatomy at the University. It was not long before he was known throughout Peru as the most noted scientific man in the country. The School of Medicine which he founded one hundred and thirty years ago is a part of the National University today. He was noted not alone for his knowledge of medicine. He knew many languages and the literature of many countries. He helped to edit a paper and wrote much of the early life of the countries, of the Inca ruins, and the music and folklore of the Indians.

Anxious for his country to progress, he worked for better methods of agriculture and mining and was able to give the people helpful advice in irrigation methods. Unanue was particularly interested in education and believed that all children, rich or poor, Indian or white, should be able to get an education. But schools were expensive, so Unanue worked out a plan by which the older children were to help teach the younger ones. For, he said, if the children who were growing up then were not educated, they would be unable to appreciate the freedom when it was finally won.

The country was making progress through Unanue's efforts when the movement for independence spread through the Americas. At first he refused to join the rebels and worked for government reforms. Later, when Spain refused to give the colonists the same political rights which Spaniards enjoyed, Unanue joined the rebels and worked as hard for independence as he had in other lines. San Martin chose him for Minister of Finance when he set up a cabinet in Lima. Later when Bolivar became President of Peru, he kept Unanue on in his same post. It was Unanue who helped Bolivar draw up Peru's first constitution. No task was too difficult and no sacrifice too great for Unanue to perform for his country. When he was seventy years old he retired to his plantation and later died there.

The Peruvians point with pride to their national hero—a famous scientist, wise statesman, learned scholar and skilled physician.

José Bonifacio, the one Portuguese member of the Gallery of Patriots, spent little time in Brazil, the country which honors him. He was born in São Paulo, Brazil, in 1763 and was educated in the schools there and in Rio de Janeiro. When he was a young man he went to Portugal to enter the University, where he was particularly interested in science. His good record as a student attracted the attention of the government and when he finished his course he was sent by the government to travel throughout Europe to gather material on science. Bonifacio had a pleasing personality and that as well as his high intelligence won him many friends among the leaders of Europe. When he returned to Portugal he did a great deal of helpful work in improving agriculture and soils.

But when Napoleon marched into Portugal, Bonifacio proved that he was as good a soldier as he was a student and scientist. He laid aside his books and led a student force from the University against the invader. Then, when the war was over, he went back to his desk and his scientific work. It was not until he was fifty-eight years old that he returned to Brazil, his own country. He had wanted to go on with his scientific work, but he was soon involved with the affairs of his country in their efforts to keep their independence. For, unlike the Spanish colonies, Brazil had been recognized as an independent empire and the King of Portugal had ruled the nation when he fled from Portugal. When the King returned to Portugal he left his son Dom Pedro in his place. Trouble broke out when Portugal tried once more to take the country under its wing. But finally the mother country recognized Brazil as an independent empire in 1825. She was saved the long, hard struggle to gain her independence which the Spanish colonies suffered, but disorder within the country followed.

It was into this trouble that Bonifacio was plunged when he returned to Brazil. For a while he held the position of Minister of the Interior and of Foreign Affairs. He was forced to resign at the end of that time by the people who opposed him. Later he was exiled for his own opposition to the policies of the cabinet and lived in France for five years. When he returned he was appointed tutor for Dom Pedro's little son, who was being educated to fill the post of emperor of Brazil some day. But again people became jealous of Bonifacio's position and sent him to a little island in the harbor of Rio de Janeiro.

For several years—until his death in 1838—the man whom Brazil was later to choose as national hero lived on the tiny island within a few miles of his country but forbidden to return to it. José Bonifacio was a poet, a scientist of note, an educator, a soldier, and a wise statesman.

Twenty years before the flag of Spain was hauled down in South America, Haiti was already an independent nation. On New Year's Day in 1804, Haiti declared her independence of France, and was the first of the Latin American republics to become an independent nation. The man chosen as the first president, Jean Jacques Dessalines, is also that country's choice for national hero.

The deeds of Toussaint l'Ouverture and Henri Christophe, who made himself king, are better known than those of Dessalines. Born a slave on a plantation, little if any record is left of his boyhood days. He was first heard of when his people rose up in 1791 and demanded the end of slavery. Two years later slavery was abolished. But the struggle did not end there and for five years the Negroes fought desperately to keep the freedom they had struggled so hard to win. It was the great Toussaint l'Ouverture who first led his people, but Dessalines fought with him so bravely that he was made a general. The forces under him were so strong that France became alarmed and Napoleon's brother-in-law, with an expedition of 25,000 men, was sent to crush them. The battles that followed are some of the most horrible in history. Thousands of lives were lost, homes were destroyed and fields laid waste. Finally, the French tricked and seized Toussaint and sent him to France where he later died in chains.

The Haitians feared lest the French would make them slaves once more and again revolted, this time under Dessalines. Yellow fever fought on the side of the rebels this time, and thousands of the French died of the disease. Finally they gave up and sailed back to France.

The Haitians declared their independence and chose Dessalines to head the new government. But Dessalines was dissatisfied with being merely a president when Napoleon was an emperor. So a few months later he changed his title to emperor. But even the high-sounding title did not make Dessalines a good head for the country. Although he had been a good soldier and fought bravely, nothing in his experience fitted him to govern a country. Two years after he became president, a revolution broke out and he was shot.

Today Haiti honors the man who rose from slave to emperor by placing him in the Gallery of Patriots.

Next door to Haiti, the Dominican Republic has chosen Juan Pablo Duarte to take his place in the Gallery of Patriots as their national hero. The memory of Duarte lives on in his country not for his work to free the country from Spanish rule, but through his efforts to throw off the rule of Haiti. No sooner was Spain's rule overthrown in this island country than Haiti took it over. For twenty-two years it suffered the sting of being ruled by its smaller neighbor.

HOUSE OF THE ADMIRALS, DOMINICAN REPUBLIC

Juan Duarte was only eight years old when Haiti seized the rule of his country. From his early primary school days through his youthful days in a school in Spain, he thought of freeing his country. "God, Liberty, and the Fatherland" was the motto of the revolutionary society which he founded when he returned from Spain. Although the members met in secret, it was not long before all the young men of the country were ready to take up arms to win their independence. Their greatest allies were finally the Haitians themselves who revolted against their cruel president. Later Duarte had to flee the country when the Haitian president led his troops into Santo Domingo. But when the Haitians were finally driven from the country, Duarte was called back to be his country's first president.

Then disorder within the Dominican Republic forced him into exile a second time. Once more he returned to help his country when Spain took it in 1864. The leaders were jealous of him because he was so well loved and this time he was exiled for the rest of his life. The man who had done so much for his country died in Venezuela a poor and unhappy man.

On Lincoln's Birthday, more than a century ago, a poor government employee and his wife carried their tiny boy baby to church to be baptized. "We shall call him José," they said. José Martí, national hero of Cuba, was born in a humble home. The teacher in the little neighborhood school where he first went to school pulled little José's ears whenever he got into mischief. Later, when he was a grown man, Martí said that he would never forget the teacher because his ears which stood away from his head reminded him of her. When he was nine years old he entered another school and easily earned the place at the head of his class as well as all of the prizes given for scholarship. José liked to study and was happy at school until his father decided he had enough education and put him to work in an office. A friend gave him money to enroll in a night school. But his employer gave him little encouragement and said it was not necessary for him to know more than he did to fill his position. When he was still a young boy he met many of his countrymen who were working for independence. Martí was an eloquent speaker and wherever groups discussed the problems of the country, his voice was raised above the others. Once when he was making an earnest speech about his country's wrongs, a map of the island fell and struck him on his head. One of the boys in the audience said: "It was as though his entire country was stirred by what he said and answered his cry." With others Martí began publication of a paper and his first poem ever published appeared in this. Years later when he was a great poet, he still remembered his happiness at seeing his poem in print. His parents did not praise him, however; instead they punished him severely because they did not agree with the ideas of independence contained in the poem.

When he was only seventeen years old he was thrown into prison with other rebels and spent several months there. Finally he was sent to Spain where he lived miserably on the small amount of money he could earn teaching.

When Martí was exiled from his country a second time he went to New York, and for the next fourteen years worked tirelessly to organize the movement for the independence of Cuba. He did all sorts of jobs. He worked as a bookkeeper, translated English and French novels for a publishing company, was a correspondent for Latin American newspapers, and edited three others. He spoke often and brilliantly before clubs and societies. He also published his books of verse which earned him a high place among poets of Latin America.

No matter what hardships he met, he never once gave up the idea of a free Cuba. The revolution was finally under way and Martí landed in Cuba and joined the army. His general pleaded with him to return to New York and keep up the work he had been doing. Martí insisted, however, on taking part in at least one battle and it was in this one that he was killed. Although he did not live to see his country free, the others carried on his work which finally gave the island its independence. On Cuba's independence day, May 20, Martí's statue, standing in a little square overlooking the sea in Havana, wears a wreath and is banked high with flowers placed there by his countrymen.

Under the leadership of a parish priest, José Matias Delgado, Central America first took up the struggle for independence. José was born in 1767 in El Salvador, which now claims him as "father of his country" and its national hero. As a boy he was educated in San Salvador, then went to Guatemala City to finish his education for the priesthood. When he had completed his studies he returned to his country and worked untiringly among his people, who were glad to follow him in the fight for independence. The first revolt in 1811 was unsuccessful, and Father Delgado was sent to Guatemala City where he was closely watched. Finally Spain's rule in the colonies was broken in 1821, and Father Delgado was made president of the government in San Salvador. When the new republics decided to unite under Mexico's rule, Father Delgado refused to join. Salvador, smallest of all the Central American nations, fought bravely against the large Mexican army sent in to conquer it, but the small army was defeated. The same year the Central Americans declared their independence from Mexico and Father Delgado was chosen president of the constitutional assembly.

The story is told that his city of San Salvador was surrounded by several different enemy troops. Supplies had run out, and only a few defenders were left. It seemed impossible to think that they could hold out much longer. But Father Delgado ordered the few tired soldiers to fire faster than before; he had others ring the church bells and set off all the fireworks they could find. The volley of shots, clanging church bells, and the fireworks bursting in the air sounded like victory to the enemies and they retreated and the city was saved.

Father Delgado alone of the national heroes of Central America had an active part in the struggle to overthrow Spain. The other men in the Gallery of Patriots were placed there for service to their countries in the difficult years following independence. Of these Francisco Morazan, national hero of Honduras, is one of the best known.

Francisco was born in 1792 in Tegucigalpa. He was educated by a tutor and was particularly fond of drawing and geometry. He was anxious to learn and whenever he could he slipped into groups and listened to the conversation of the learned men of the town. He had a pleasant personality and easily made friends. When he was sixteen years old his family moved to a small town where the only educated men were the judge and the secretary of the town council. Because Francisco was always polite and cheerful, they let him do odd jobs about their office in his spare time. It wasn't long, however, before they began to ask his opinion on many of their problems.

He began his service for his country six years after Central America had won her independence from Spain. Morazan led the forces of his country against troops from Guatemala which came to overthrow the liberal government in Honduras. But he was defeated. He organized another force and this time defeated the enemy. The fighting continued off and on and finally Morazan was made president of the Central American Federation. Once he was exiled to Peru but came back to Central America in answer to the call of the people of Costa Rica who asked him to help free them from the dictator who ruled them. He landed at the west coast of Costa Rica and won over the army who came to meet him without firing a shot. He was elected president of Costa Rica, but was shot and killed when he tried again to restore the federation.

"You can't even read" was the taunt thrown at a fourteen-year-old boy in Guatemala who loved to play war and ride wild ponies instead of studying his lessons. But that day Justo Rufino Barrios vowed that no one would ever be able to say that to him again. He looked up a tutor and set himself to the task of learning to read with the same determination with which he stuck to the backs of his ponies. His parents were delighted to see the boy, who had given them so much trouble as a child, settle down to his studies. They encouraged him in every way and sent him on to higher schools and finally to Guatemala City where he graduated in law in 1862. Young Rufino came from a well-to-do family, but he hated the way the poor boys in the University were treated. He rebelled against the aristocratic government of his country and its disregard of the common people. From the time he left school he began the struggle which finally placed him at the head of his government. Barrios was always ambitious for his country and built railways, telegraph communications, and hospitals, and wrote wise laws. Nor did the boy who had neglected his studies as a child forget to build schools for his country. One dream he kept always before him. He wished to see the five countries of Central America united as one country. But once he began to work for the union he saw that it would never be accomplished peacefully. Because he was so determined, he decided to build it by force. Riding from the capital at the head of his troops, he led them against the troops sent from El Salvador. But in a battle fought on April 2, 1885, Barrios was killed. Justo Rufino Barrios, national hero of Guatemala, and often called "The Reformer," has been described as a combination of Abraham Lincoln, Theodore Roosevelt, and Pancho Villa.

Juan Rafael Mora was only six years old when Spain's rule in the colonies was finally broken. Born into a poor Costa Rican family, he had little chance to attend school and when he was still very young he went to work to help support his family. Just before his death, his father lost the little money he had and young Mora had the difficult task of looking after his two brothers and seven sisters, as well as paying off his father's debts. He was a hard worker and had the satisfaction of finally paying all the money his father owed.

Mora was particularly interested in agriculture and it was on his plantation that the first coffee was grown in Costa Rica. In 1847 he was elected Vice President of his country and two years later moved up to the presidency. His efforts in bringing about the defeat of William Walker in Nicaragua won for Mora his place as national hero of his country. While he was president, Costa Rica had one of its most prosperous periods. Remembering, perhaps, the little opportunity he had to go to school when he was a child, Mora built many primary schools and also founded schools of medicine and law.

Among the soldiers who fought so bravely with General Sucre in the famous battle of Ayacucho in Peru was a nineteen-year-old lieutenant. Born in Panama City, Tomas Herrera fought first to break the rule of Spain in the colonies. When independence was finally won, his country joined the Republic of

Photo by Ewing Galloway, N. Y.

MORRO CASTLE, CUBA

Colombia. It was not long before groups in Panama began to work for separation from Colombia. General Herrera was one of the guiding spirits in the movement and in 1840 the little country broke away from Colombia. But the success was brief and in thirteen months the country was again a part of Colombia. Although Panama did not become an independent nation until 1903, it has chosen for its national hero the man who led it to its brief victory in 1840 and was named its president. Four years later, he was made governor of Panama, and under his wise leadership the country progressed. Later in Colombia he was made governor of the Province of Cartagena. He even held the high office of president of the country when the president and vice president were absent. Here Herrera proved himself as brave as when he fought with Sucre. When the government was threatened, he succeeded in driving the enemy from Bogotá, the capital, and restoring the government. But the wounds he received in the battle cost him his life, and he died as his victorious army marched into the city.

In the Gallery of Patriots a full-blooded Zapotec Indian shares a place with the great men chosen by the American Republics as their national heroes.

It is almost a century and a half since a little Indian boy first played in his highland village in Mexico. Few who saw Benito Juarez then would have believed that this brown-faced, wiry boy would one day be a match for kings and emperors. They could not know then that years after his death not only his country but the world would remember and respect him. He was still a very young child when his parents died. But later a kindly priest in Oaxaca took Benito and educated him. It was in the classes he attended there that he first learned Spanish. He liked to study, and spent long hours poring over books from his guardian's library. In 1834, when he was twenty-eight years old, he finished his law course.

His country had gained its independence from Spain, but its rule had fallen to the wealthy, aristocratic class. The rest of the nation had little, if any, more freedom than they had under the Spanish flag. It was against the government of this class that Juarez early began his fight. "The Mexican Lincoln" he has been called, for he fought for the same ideals that Lincoln fought for in this country. Juarez carried on his fight against the poverty and ignorance which held the peasants of his country in virtual slavery. He fought for his people's voice in government, but he realized that without education they could not take their place in a democracy.

In 1857 Juarez was made Chief Justice of the Supreme Court of Mexico. He was next in line for the presidency, but when the president was forced out of office the following year, another president took the office and Juarez had to leave the capital. Then began his long, hard years of struggle in which he led his troops from one end of the country to another. Sometimes defeat seemed certain. Several times his own lieutenants turned against him. But no matter what the discouragements, Juarez never gave up the fight, and four years later he led his troops into Mexico City. He immediately began to put reform laws into effect. But the country was poor and there was little money in the treasury and none to pay the foreign countries

Photo by Ewing Galloway, N.Y.

PYRAMID OF THE SUN NEAR MEXICO CITY

from whom Mexico had borrowed. It was then that Maximilian of Austria was sent to Mexico to take over the rule with himself as emperor.

Once again Juarez and his troops had long, hard years of bitter fighting. But in 1867 he was able to take over the government of his country and remained its president until he died in 1872.

This man whom Mexico has chosen as her national hero was tireless in his fight for democracy.

In 1940, representatives of the American nations met in the Gallery of Patriots to place a wreath beneath the bust of Colombia's hero, Francisco de Paula Santander.

Santander was born on April 12, 1792, of a wealthy family. He finished his legal studies in 1810 and at once joined the independence movement. His unusual military skill in recruiting and training armies earned him the title "The Organizer of Victory." He served with distinction in the army for nine years and then while Bolivar finished his task of liberator, Santander took over the work of government. Today Colombia honors him for his work in organizing schools and courts of justice and in developing national industries.

When Bolivar returned to Colombia to assume the presidency, Santander remained as vice-president. Accused of taking part in an attempted assassination of Bolivar, Santander was banished from Colombia. He spent his exile in Europe and the United States and returned to Colombia after Bolivar's death. In 1832 he was elected president for a five-year term. He died May 6, 1840.

These seventeen * men in the Gallery of Patriots fought bravely to win their nation's independence and peace from the disorders that followed.

In each of the American Republics equally brave men have carried on the fight in other fields to keep the independence won for them on the battlefield. Among them are great educators, skilled doctors, wise lawyers, gifted writers, and eloquent orators. All share a place in the memories of the Americas.

* Ecuador, Nicaragua, and Paraguay have not yet chosen their national heroes for a place in the Gallery of Patriots.

THE AMERICAS AT A GLANCE *

Country	Population	Area in Square Miles	Capital
Argentina	12,761,611	1,079,965	Buenos Aires
Bolivia	2,911,283	419,470	La Paz
Brazil	44,002,095	3,286,170	Rio de Janeiro
Chile	4,585,705	286,396	Santiago
Colombia	8,665,000	476,916	Bogotá
Costa Rica	606,581	23,000	San José
Cuba	4,108,650	44,164	Habana
Dominican Republic	1,581,248	19,325	Ciudad Trujillo
Ecuador	2,554,744	undetermined	Quito
El Salvador	1,631,967	13,183	San Salvador
Guatemala	2,266,682	48,290	Guatemala City
Haiti	3,000,000	10,700	Port-au-Prince
Honduras	962,685	46,332	Tegucigalpa
Mexico	16,552,722	760,372	Mexico, D. F.
Nicaragua	638,119	49,200	Managua
Panama	547,536	34,170	Panama
Paraguay	1,000,000	154,165	Asunción
Peru	6,147,000	undetermined	Lima
Uruguay	2,082,367	72,153	Montevideo
Venezuela	3,451,677	393,976	Caracas
United States	132,597,800	3,738,395 †	Washington, D. C.

* FROM "THE AMERICAS, A PANORAMIC VIEW," PAN AMERICAN UNION, WASHINGTON, D. C., 1939.

† INCLUDES POSSESSIONS AND TERRITORIES.

INDEX

298

302